Youth Gone Wild

Robert "Bob" Sorensen

First Edition

Fulton Books, Inc.
Meadville, PA

Published by Fulton Books 2020

ISBN 978-1-64654-349-6 (paperback)
ISBN 978-1-64654-350-2 (digital)

Printed in the United States of America

We do not remember days; we remember moments.

—Unknown

The Beginning

June 25, 1961, a beautiful baby girl is born. She is named Karen. She is the firstborn child of Emil (Bud) and Joan Sorensen. She is perfect in every way—beautiful light-brown hair, dark-blue eyes, and soft white skin. The young couple, married two years prior, cannot be happier. All they've thought of, all they've talked about since taking their wedding vows was to start a family. How could you possibly ask for a better start?

Joan, the only daughter of Joseph and Adelaide Gabrick, was born and raised in a small Central Illinois town called Toluca. She has an older brother (Joseph) and a younger brother (James). They are all very close. Because she is the only girl in the family, she is constantly doted on; one might even say spoiled. She is pretty, intelligent, and extremely personable. She would go on to graduate from High School as the valedictorian of her class of sixteen. Upon graduation, she would move to the big city (Chicago) to make her mark in the world. She would become a secretary, be active in local/national politics, and frequent the jazz clubs on the weekend. Somewhere in the near future, she would meet my father, go through a relatively short courting/engagement period, and get married. From that point on, she would become known to my father as his "country girl."

Emil, one of three sons of Emil and Sue Sorensen, was born and raised in the Chicagoland area. He has an older brother (George) and an identical twin brother (Don). George was a big burly kid who grew up defending his twin brothers. He was their protector. If anybody messed with either of them, George would kick ass and take names later. The twins were small frail boys. Starting at an early age, my grandmother would dress them up in identical outfits; many of which were quite feminine in nature. Many a times, people would comment on what cute girls they were. Thank God for Uncle George. The beautiful thing about being a twin was always having someone to be there as you go through all the stages of life—grade school, high school. They were both drafted into the Army at the same time. They both were stationed at the same army base (thank God they never saw any action). They were both discharged at the same time, going off to college (University of Illinois) on the GI Bill, earning degrees in architecture. They applied for the same job (drafter) at the same employer, working the same set hours in the same office area. The die was set at birth and would continue through the death of my Uncle Don. Emil, shortly after establishing himself in the workforce, he met my mother, fell in love, and got married. My mother found her "city boy."

My parents set up house in a two-flat on the northwest side of the city, which they called Mackley's Mansion. A small two-bedroom apartment across the street from St. Ladislaus School (where I would eventually attend school) and Chopin Park (the site of many of my future escapades). One of those bedrooms was painted a beautiful light-pink with a ballet dancer border.

Upon Karen's arrival from the hospital, she would spend her first two months in a cradle next to my parents' bed. After those two months were over, she would transition into this beautiful girl's bedroom—pink sheets/comforter, pretty stuffed animals of all kinds, a baby duck and lamb mobile hanging above the crib. A perfect environment for this pretty little girl to begin her life. My parents were so proud of Karen—the girl of their dreams. My father went out and bought an 8 mm camera to capture every moment of Karen's development. In addition to that, my parents would take her to a photo studio every ninety days to get professional pictures taken of her to gladly share with all their friends and family. Life was good.

Tuesday, November 6, 1962, Election Day, a four-pound, two-ounce baby boy is born at St. Anne's Hospital in Chicago, Illinois. He is eight weeks premature and is immediately moved into an incubator in the ICU, where he will spend the next two months of his life. He is very small. He is very frail. At a point very early on, a priest is brought in to issue the last rites to this tiny boy. No one is sure if he is going to survive or not. The baby's name is Robert, the firstborn son of Emil and Joan. What a way for me to enter this earth. A far cry from my sister's entrance. Instead of going home to a beautiful blue nursery, I am lying in a box, under a heat lamp, with a respirator helping me to breathe. Sterile white walls. Unfamiliar faces coming and going. Which one is my mother? No time for bonding with your mother when you're fighting for your survival. Insult to injury. The doctors tell my mother the reason I was prematurely born is a direct result of her smoking cigarettes throughout her pregnancy.

Back in the '50s and '60s, smoking was the thing to do. Doctors went on radio and television to tell people how good and healthy smoking was for you. Tell that to my mother as she raises my head with her finger. Tell that to me as I fight for my life—my lungs, my nerves, my eyes not fully developed. After several months of touch and go, I am now healthy enough to be released from the hospital. In anticipation of my arrival home, Karen is moved into a kid-sized bed in the corner of the room, making space in her old crib for yours truly. Everything remains the same—pink walls, pink sheets, ducks and lambs. Little did I know then that this would be a pattern followed by my mother for years to come. She was not prepared to raise a boy. She had not been exposed to this type of environment. That said, she was going to go with what she knew. She was going to raise her oldest son exactly the way she raised her oldest daughter. In a nutshell, I was screwed from the get-go—prematurely born, no time to bond with your mother early on in life, going to be raised like a little girl. God help me!

*****

Since my arrival on this planet, it became quite apparent, due to my premature birth, that I would not be the "perfect" child like my oldest sister Karen was. My nerves were not fully developed, making me a very hyperactive and sensitive child. I was crying, screaming, and active all the time. Morning, noon, and night. Sleep was nonexistent. My lungs were not fully developed, so I had a hard time breathing. In between my crying jags, I would be gasping for breath. My mother was at a loss, panicked all the time. I spent many hours in the bathroom with the hot water running (steam). The vaporizer ran in my room constantly. An industrial-sized jar of Vicks VapoRub sat next to the crib, applied generously day and night. In addition, my eye muscles were not fully developed, resulting in a lazy eye. I was a real mess of a child. This was not what my parents signed up for. Needless to say, the 8 mm camera did not come out often with me in the picture. Who wanted to take movies of a screaming, cross-eyed baby? For obvious reasons, we never did make it to the photo studio as well. You would never get me to stop crying and sit still enough to take a decent picture. No sense of wasting anyone's time and money. Looking back, we have hours upon hours of movies of Karen and beautiful pictures of her from the photo studios. Me? An occasional picture of this wild child peeking out from under his pink blanket. What a mess. What a way to start out my life.

Shortly after my arrival, my parents decided they needed more space to raise their growing family. We had outgrown our little apartment. As fortune might have it, my father was able to find and purchase a four-bedroom bungalow five houses north of our existing location. Two months later, the four of us moved into our new home on Roscoe Street. Perfect. Still across the street from Chopin Park.

Walking distance from the school. As my parents set up shop, the decision had to be made on where to locate the two children. The way the house was set up, there were two bedrooms on the main floor, one being the master bedroom (for my parents) and the other bedroom right down the hall, separated by a bathroom. The other two bedrooms were upstairs, separated by a small hallway. Common sense would tell you to put the youngest child (me) in the bedroom closest to my parents, putting Karen in one of the bedrooms upstairs. Unfortunately, common sense did not prevail in this case (as we get further into this book, you will see that it never did prevail). Once again, the pink paint and wallpaper came out, and Karen's room was decorated to perfection. What more could a little girl ask for?

As for me, I was located in the bigger of the two bedrooms upstairs. Mind you, the bedrooms upstairs were semifinished (loft in nature)—tiled floors, bare wood ceilings (slanting down from the center, following the pitch of the roof). There was a lone window at the far end of the room. Very dark. Very cold. Very barren. Just the place for a young boy to begin the next phase of his life. Where were my blue walls? Where was my teddy bear border? For the life of me, I could never figure out what was going through my parents' minds at the time of this decision. I missed out bonding with my mom when I was first born. Having me close to them at this point might have made up for some of this lost time. The best I could figure was, they wanted the "devil child" as far away from them as possible. Much harder to hear me screaming/crying upstairs than it would be right down the hall from their bedroom. Could sleep be more important than bonding with your son? I guess I got my answer. Again, I was too young at the time to know what was happening. Looking back, I can now see the wheels were put in motion at an early age, resulting in some of the stories I will be sharing with you later on in this book. A note to any and all parents reading this book. It's true. Those early years with your children are so important to their future growth and development. The seeds are planted early. Make sure you continue to sow them over the years.

*****

So it goes. As my sister Karen continued to bond with my parents in her gender-appropriate room, I continued to languish in my cold, dark cell. A few more tidbits on my surroundings before I move on. Seeing my father was the sole provider (as was typical of the time, my mother did not work for many years) and having just moved into a new home, my parents did not have a lot of expendable income. What little they had was spent on things they deemed necessary—a new bed for Karen's room, a new television set (my dad was addicted to TV), a new dining room table and chairs. Anything and everything that was needed to keep up the facade to all who entered the Sorensen home, that we were this happy, loving family, that we really had our shit together. Seeing my father was an architect, everything at the time had to be based on design rather than comfort or functionality. In his mind, he was going to be the next Frank Lloyd Wright.

With money being spent on the main floor of the house, unfortunately, my bedroom upstairs was an afterthought. It would be best described as an army barracks. In two of the four corners of the room lie twin beds left over from the previous owners. Being so young, I had no idea of the age of these beds. Based on the fact they would almost touch the ground when you lay on them, I'm guessing they were pretty damn old. As I described earlier, the ceilings were slanted based on the pitch of the roof. That said, you had approximately eighteen inches from the top of the mattress to the ceiling. Have a bad dream in the middle of the night, crack your skull. Wake up in the morning disoriented, crack your skull. Mom screams up the stairs that it's time for breakfast, crack your skull. You get the gist of it. No curtains on the windows. No pictures or artwork of any kind on the walls. There was a dim, broken-down light on the far end of the room attached to a light switch at the entryway. The only time this switch was used was when my mother left the room in the evening, thrusting me into total darkness. Underneath the curtainless windows, my father placed a homemade table—a flat piece of plywood with four metal legs, unfinished, unpainted. Certainly fit in quite well in its surroundings. This was my room. This was where I'd spend my childhood. This was where I'd spend my teenage years.

It became quite apparent, at an early age, that my mother was not programmed to raise a baby boy. Karen was such a well-behaved child. Karen looked beautiful in her little dresses and pantsuits. Here was this hyperactive, goofy-looking Tasmanian devil of a child. I'm sure my mother was asking herself, *What can I do with this child?* The answer was quite simple. Raise him like you did Karen. If she came out so good, applying the same logic to me would reap the same benefits. Almost immediately, my mom started using my sister's hand-me-down clothes to dress me in. Certainly not dresses, but anything else was fair game. There were many a childhood picture of me—red-faced, tears rolling down my cheeks, me screaming like a banshee in a flowered onesie. The balance of my clothes, bought at our local department stores (JCPenney, Sears, Goldblatt's, etc.), were not much better—little sailor suits, goofy-looking puffy pirate shirts. I was in big trouble.

I should mention something at this point. Because my father was a twin, my Grandma Sorensen really doted on him and his brother. They were what one might call Momma's boys. Unfortunately, his mother subjected him to the same type of "abuse" as my mother was putting me through—little Emil and Donnie in their matching sailor suits. Bottom line, I could never count on my father (or my grandmother for that matter) to step in and provide my mother with proper guidance to raise a baby boy. They considered this "normal" behavior. The only person I could count on at this time in my life was my Grandpa Sorensen. He was a big, burly, speaks-his-mind kind of guy. He saw what was happening. He tried to step in and put a stop to this madness. Unfortunately, he was married to a hot-headed Italian woman who would shut him down in a heartbeat. I will say this. The only normal clothes from my childhood came from him. A little Chicago Cubs uniform, along with a matching hat. A cowboy outfit consisting of a tinted flannel shirt and blue jeans (including a cap gun and holster). He must have figured he missed out on his sons, so he was going to try to save me. Thank you, Grandpa! I will never forget you for that.

*****

As I grew older, my parents hoped and prayed I would grow out of my "naughty" behavior. What they didn't realize back then that is so prevalent now was the fact that I was suffering from a severe case of ADHD. Very few people, including my parents, had any idea how to deal with this type of behavior back in the '60s. The only way they knew back then was to scream, yell, and punish. Whenever I had one of my tantrums, my mother would grab me by my shoulders, scream in my face, spank my bottom, and banish me to my room. Of course, that would incense me even more. I would scream, yell, and cry for hours (until, in most cases, I would lose my voice). When that didn't have any impact, I would sit in the corner of my room and bang my head against the wall. Over and over. Harder and harder. My mom would rush up the stairs, yell at me to stop, and then head back down. As soon as she was gone, I would start all over again. It is amazing I didn't damage my vocal cords or suffer any permanent brain damage (some may argue that I have!).

Along with these consistent outbursts came destruction. I would destroy anything in my wake. As I sat at my lone window, looking at the kids playing in the park, I would punch holes in my window screen. When my dad would eventually get around to fixing it, I would do the exact same thing again and again and again. Any toy left in my room was fair game. I'd pull the eyes and the arms off my teddy bears. I'd tear the pages out of my books. I'd pull off every wheel from my Matchbox cars, Tonka trucks, etc. I had so much pent-up energy this was the only way I knew how to get it out. One story in particular that stood out was almost surreal. For God knows what reason, my parents decided to buy me a dart board and hang it in my room. We are not talking about the metal kind with magnets.

We are talking about a corkboard with real darts (the sharp, pointed metal kind). Again, what were they thinking? Throwing the darts at the board was fun for the first five to ten minutes. Once I realized these darts would stick in the surrounding wood walls, the game was on! Getting banished to my room on a daily basis was no longer an issue. I would spend hours upon hours randomly firing those darts into the surrounding walls. What fun! Once I bored of this activity, my overactive mind came up with another idea.

Growing up in the city (especially living across the street from a public park), we were subjected to all types of graffiti. The kind that intrigued me the most at this very young age were the messages scrawled into the park benches. "Johnny loves Mary." "Steve's a pothead." They were there for everyone to see, there for eternity. I said to myself, "How cool will it be for me to leave my mark in this world just like all these other folks are doing!" That said, I took one of my darts, walked out into the hallway between the upstairs bedrooms, and as deep and as hard as I could push, I wrote, "Bob was here," with an arrow point to the spot where I was standing. I thought it was the most beautiful thing in the world. My parents did not agree. In response, my dart board and darts were removed from my room and an eye hook was placed on the outside of my bedroom door. From this point on, when I was sent to my room for doing something wrong (almost daily), the eye hook was latched, and I was locked in, unable to leave until my mother undid the hook. Needless to say, this drove me even more insane. The screaming, yelling, and head pounding intensified. I really did feel like a prisoner in my own room.

*****

February 24, 1966, my younger sister Laura is born. She, like my older sister, is a beautiful, healthy baby girl. By this point, my mother had stopped smoking for several years, so there were no complications or birth defects. In advance of her arrival, my parents updated the bedroom across the hallway from mine to move Karen—beautiful red curtains with matching bed spread; big, fluffy, colorful pillows positioned throughout; a store-bought desk-and-chair set, perfect for a little girl to sit and play with her dollies. Karen's downstairs bedroom was repainted and decorated in advance of Laura's arrival. Meanwhile, I continued to languish in my "holding cell." Nothing had changed in my room. I take partial responsibility for this situation. Anything new introduced into this environment was immediately destroyed by me. From my parent's perspective, I could understand why you wouldn't want to spend good money after bad. So it goes.

At this point, I want to fast-forward a year. It's the summer of 1967. There are several distinct memories I would like to share with you from this period. In June, my sister Karen celebrated her sixth birthday. My parents threw her a beautiful friends and family party. She was so excited and so happy. After the party was over, everyone was asked to head outside for the *big surprise.* Sitting in the front yard was the most beautiful girl's bike you would every want to see—metallic red with white pinstripes, a big white seat, tassels hanging from each of the handlebars. The icing on the cake? A battery-powered headlamp that you control with an on/off switch. It was probably the most beautiful thing I had ever seen in my short time on this planet. Don't ask me what compelled me to do what I did next. I could not explain my actions other than I was a four-year-old boy suffering from untreated ADHD, pissed off that my sister was the center of attention once again. I broke through the crowd and jumped on the bike. I proceeded to pedal as hard as I could. At my age, I had never been on a two-wheeled bike. That said, I immediately lost control of the bike and slammed it into the nearest tree. The front wheel and rim immediately folded up, taking the beautiful headlamp with it. The bike was destroyed. My sister was crying. My parents were screaming. All the guests were shaking their heads, trying to figure out what just happened. Me? I was so proud of myself that I was able to control a two-wheeled bike for almost ten feet. What was all the commotion about? Needless to say, I was banished to my room for the balance of the day, eye hook in place.

Later that summer, my parents decided to take a driving vacation to California. Seeing Laura was still a baby, my folks dropped her off at the house of my mother's parents and headed west. We got as far as Nebraska that day. My father got a hotel room for the evening. *Oh my god, they have an in-ground pool!* I'd seen these kinds of pools on TV but never in person. The only pools we'd seen in person were the ones with the three rings that you blew up in the backyard. Maybe twelve inches of water to piddle around in. This was a real pool with deep dark-blue water (from the painted surface). I could no longer contain my excitement. As my parents were unloading Karen and the luggage from the car into the room, I'd decided it was time to go for a swim. I immediately bolted for the pool at full stride. No need to switch into my swimming suit. Who cares if I don't know how to swim? I jumped straight into the deep end of the pool. Of course, I went straight down to the bottom like a rock. My dad, who was quite a few paces behind me at this point, eventually caught up, jumped in fully clothed, and brought me back to the surface. Tragedy averted. In my mind, it was the coolest thing I'd ever seen or done. Not once did I stop and think how dangerous this was, how I could have killed myself.

Fast-forward a week. My parents decided, for whatever reason, to take us to Hearst Castle in San Simeon, California. For those of you not familiar with the area, the castle is a historic landmark, set on the cliffs overlooking the Pacific Ocean. Each room is filled with priceless antiques from all over the world. Our visit was well before any of today's restrictions that we are so accustomed to. No ropes. No gates. As we entered the grounds, I immediately saw the beautiful pools stretching out for yards in front of us. I made a run for it. This time, my dad was ready. He scooped me up from behind and held me under his arms as we continued to tour the grounds. Of course, I was kicking and screaming the whole time. It was now time to head inside the castle. I was like a kid in a candy store. All these bright, beautiful objects, I wanted to touch them all. I wanted to play with them. I went wild. My mom was holding my hand tight—so tight I could feel the circulation being cut off. The harder she squeezed, the harder I pulled. After fifteen to twenty minutes of this tug-of-war, my parents decided to abort the mission. Prior to heading back to the car, my parents decided to take a look at the Pacific Ocean. We headed west toward the cliffs. As we got closer, I got more excited. My parents must have seen it in my eyes. I wanted nothing more than to run off those cliffs! I had no fear. There was no hesitation. This time, each of my parents had a hold of one of my hands. Over their dead bodies were they going to let their son run off a five-hundred-foot cliff, falling to his death. I share these stories with you, the reader, to give you a clear understanding of my mind-set as a child. I'm hyperactive. I'm fearless. I'm being dressed and raised as a little girl. I've spent half my life in solitary confinement. Is it any wonder what comes next?

*****

September 1967, my mom could not control her excitement. It was the first day of kindergarten, meaning she would have four hours a day, five days a week away from her crazy son. A much-needed break after almost five years of nonstop crying, screaming, mayhem, and destruction. She had spent the last several weeks preparing for this day—numerous trips to the store to pick out my new go-to school clothing. Blue jeans? T-shirts? Gym shoes? Guess again. She wanted her son looking his finest when heading off to St. Ladislaus for his first day of school. As I got dressed in my checkerboard, button-down shirt, green dress pants (commonly known as floods), and black patent leather shoes, I was extremely nervous. Seeing I had not been in contact with too many children at this point in my life (excluding siblings and cousins), I had no idea what to expect. My mother called. It was time to go. She was kind enough to walk me the half block to the front entrance of the school. That would be the last time that ever happened. She handed me off to a young woman standing on the front stoop.

"You be a big boy and be good to your teacher." No hug. No kiss. She was gone. My parents were never the touchy, feely type. Lots of talk. Very little physical contact (with the exception of spankings, which, for obvious reasons, was quite often). I was escorted into my classroom where fifteen to twenty children of all shapes, sizes, gender, and ethnicity were gathered. I was like a deer in headlights. Scared shitless. Mind you, I am only four years old at this point in my life. I will not turn five until my birthday in November. I was, by far, one of the youngest children in the class. On top of that, based on my hyperactivity, as well as healthy, well-balanced meals being served at home (junk food of any kind was prohibited by my mother), I was what you would call the runt of the litter. Add in the lazy eye, and I was a mess. Even as early as kindergarten, kids could be cruel. It did not take long for my class to break into these little cliques—the older kids, the spoiled kids, the little class clowns, the bullies. Let's not forget about the dorks. Take a guess what clique I was in?

As the year progressed, these cliques became more and more defined. My fate was set at a very early age. I was picked on by the bullies. I was made fun of by the older kids. The class clowns had a field day with me. I was miserable. I would come home every day, crying like a little schoolgirl (how appropriate), with no support from either of my parents.

"Why can't you be more like your sister Karen?"

"You need to start acting like a big boy!"

The trouble was, I was not a big boy. I was only four years old for Chrissake. Insult to injury. Right after the Christmas holiday, my parents decided it was time for me to have an eye operation to fix my lazy eye. Upon completion of that operation, I would have to wear an eye patch for several months. On top of that, I was fitted for a pair of glasses that I would have to wear for the rest of my life. No need to pick out a pair that might be remotely cool to a kid. We had to get the strongest, longest lasting pair they had. Back to school I go. Pirate patch covering my right eye. My Buddy Holly glasses firmly set on my nose. Again, the die had been set. I was, by far, the dorkiest kid you ever wanted to see. I was a very easy target. The balance of the year was even more miserable. Summer break could not come soon enough. A side note worth mentioning at this point: both my parents were pacifists. Instead of my mother talking to my teacher or my father telling me to stick up for myself (maybe even show me how to defend myself), they both told me I must try to reason with my tormentors.

"Nothing is ever solved through violence."

"Sticks and stones may break your bones, but words will never hurt you."

My ass! The more I tried to talk and the more I tried to reason, the more I got picked on and bullied. It was no use. No relief at school. No support at home.

*****

It was now the summer of 1968. By the grace of God, I survived the school year, and I had a few months off before I had to worry about first grade. I tried not to think about the horrors that await you during a full day of school. By this time, Karen had gotten her bike repaired, and she was riding like a champ. Me? I was not responsible enough to have a two-wheeled bike. I would just destroy it like everything else that was ever given to me. The solution? Let me continue to ride my sister's old three-wheeled tricycle (again, a beautiful metallic pink, with tassels and a big wide girl's seat). We would ride up and down the alley—Karen on her beautiful new bike, me on her old three-wheeler. What a pair. It was during these "adventures" that we met our first friends—Billy and Mary. Mary was in my class; Billy was a year behind.

At first, life was grand. We would all ride our bikes, back and forth, asking questions of one another to find out as much as we could about our new friends. Then things took a twist. Karen, being the oldest, became the unspoken leader of the pack. Mary and Billy did everything they could to get on her good side, be her favorite. Here we go again. First, Karen started picking on me (showing off). Then Mary and Billy jumped on board. It was three on one with the runt trying to "reason" with everyone. It was at this point in my life that I was assigned my nickname that would stay with me for the rest of my life. I am now known as Baby Bike Bob. A unique relationship was now forged between the four of us. One on one, everything was great. We talked. We played. We rode bikes. The moment the four of us were together, I was the odd man out. This relationship would go on like this for years. I accepted this behavior, saying "part-time friends" were better than no friends at all.

*****

Fast-forward to the fall of 1969. I'd survived first grade and was ready to begin second grade. I was still a skinny, hyperactive runt with my Mr. Magoo glasses. Thank God we were all wearing standard-issue school uniforms—white shirt, black pants, a little button-down bow tie, black shoes. My mom's choice in clothing for me had not changed. I'd worry about that on the weekends. We were now into the first few weeks of school and settling down into our patterns. I'd accepted my fate for the time being, and I was fine with it, until I came home one evening. My sister joined the choir the year prior, and she loved it. She came home every day after practice to tell my parents how wonderful it was. The highlight of her week was when we would go to church and see her and the rest of the choir singing up in the balcony. How beautiful for a lovely young girl. My parents came up with an excellent idea. Seeing Karen was getting so much out of this, why not have Bob join? What? There were twelve children in the choir—all girls. In the long history of the St. Ladislaus School choir, not one boy has ever joined. I went crazy—screaming, yelling, banging my head on the table, just like old times. I was sent to my room, the eye hook fastened, to think about my unacceptable behavior while my parents plot out my fate. After several hours, I was released to be informed of their decision.

"You will be joining the choir. You will be practicing every day, singing side by side with your sister every Sunday. Now get dressed. We're going down to JCPenney's to buy you some appropriate clothing."

My heart sank. My parents had to literally drag me to the car. I was kicking and screaming. As we arrived, my mom peeled off, leaving my father and me to pick out my choir outfits. As I mentioned earlier, my dad was an architect. Everything, including the clothes you wear, are about appearance. He decided at that moment that the best way to dress me was to buy clothes to the exact specifications to what he was wearing—a little mini me. A mini trench coat. A little mini sport coat. Little mini striped shirts with holes for little mini cuff links. Are you fucking kidding me? Like I don't have enough troubles as it is! As I was forced to try on all these clothes, I proceeded to throw all of them on the changing room floor. I was in a rage, crying uncontrollably. I was doing everything I could to derail this nightmare to no success. My parents paid for the clothes and headed home. It was Tuesday evening.

The next day, after school, my sister hunted me down and took me to choir practice. Even the girls were laughing at me. I couldn't cry because boys don't cry in front of girls. I stood there like a zombie, wishing I could swan dive off the balcony. As we exited the church on day 1, several of my new school friends were goofing around on the steps. They saw me and immediately put two and two together. Of course, they started riding my ass immediately. Sunday came around, and it was time to do this for real in church. My sister and I headed upstairs as the people filed in for mass. Of course, it was a full house. I was off to the side, hoping no one would see me. Right before church was scheduled to begin, the moderator made a few announcements.

"Blah, blah, blah. And finally, please welcome Robert Sorensen to the St. Ladislaus choir. We are so happy to have him!"

Holy Shit! I turned white as a ghost. As I looked down over the crowd, I saw my parents taking pictures of me in my mini-me trench coat. It felt like every set of eyes was on me. And here I thought it couldn't get any worse. Guess again.

*****

In the spring of 1970, I was scheduled to make my first Holy Communion. This is a very big deal in the Catholic church. I was so angry and bitter from the choir situation (which I was still forced to be a part of) I could barely function on a daily basis, let alone prepare for this. I went through the motions. Of course, this meant another trip to the store for a mini-me suit. As I accepted the Eucharist, I asked God why he was punishing me this way. *Will I always be the whipping boy, the punching bag, the runt?* After the ceremony, we headed back home for a family party in celebration of my communion. Now I'd been told by many of my classmates that these parties were big deals. Toys, sporting equipment, money, etc. It was like Christmas came early. My head was spinning in anticipation of what was to come. As we gathered around the table, my mother handed me a neatly wrapped rectangular box. No baseball mitt here. What could this be? I rapidly unwrapped it. It was a brown box with the word *Timex* on it. I opened it. It was a watch. It was a fucking watch! My dad then made a short speech, saying how he'd noticed I'd been admiring his and that now his little man could have one of his own.

"Bob, please take care of this as it is quite expensive and should not be played with like a toy."

Are you kidding me? My mom, all smiles, took my left arm and then placed the watch on it. I was then forced to stand there, with a fake smile, holding back my tears, as my relatives snapped picture after picture of my new watch. Once pictures were completed, everyone settled back into their seats. Me? I was so pissed off I was seeing red. As others around me talked and laughed, I was seething. I looked at the watch on my arm. A symbol of my horse shit childhood to date. I began to pick and pick at the glass cover. *Pop!* It was off. I then began to spin the exposed arms around and around. Was I trying to turn back time or fast-forward? Who knows? When I bored of that activity, I decided to snap each of the arms off, thinking I could put them back on whenever I chose. *Ping! Ping!* They were gone. I looked down at my watch, and I was so proud of myself. A few minutes later, my grandpa asked me to take another look at that "fine" watch. He stared at it, then me, in horror. He, of course, brought this to the attention of my parents, who, in response, took me upstairs, spanked the living hell out of me, and locked me in my black hole. Happy First Communion!

*****

It was now the fall of 1970. I was heading into third grade. Again, because of my height, weight, behavior, and glasses, I was an easy target for my classmates. Not a day went by without me being picked on in some form or fashion. For the time being, I accepted my fate. My attempt at "reasoning" with my bullies (per my parents' instructions) had zero impact. Later in life, I would hear a line from the movie *Caddyshack* that would perfectly describe my situation at this time: "If I saw myself in those clothes, I'd have to kick my own ass!" So true. My mom's response to all this at the time? "Let's sign you up for Cub Scouts. This will allow you to further interact with boys your own age while learning a new set of skills." Now the last thing in the world I needed right now was more interaction with the kids from school. Wasn't it enough I was getting my ass kicked from eight to three, five days a week? Add in Billy, my neighborhood "friend," and you can make that seven days a week.

I begged, pleaded, and slammed my head into the wall to no avail. She signed me up anyways.

"First, we must buy you a uniform. There is a store in the neighborhood that sells officially licensed Boy Scout uniforms."

As we headed out the door, my mom told me to behave while we were at Goldblatt's.

"Goldblatt's? Mom, why are we going there. We need to go to the uniform shop."

"Don't be silly, Bob, we can't afford to buy you your uniform from there. Goldblatt's sells uniforms at a much cheaper price."

I didn't like the sound of that. We headed out, bought a "uniform," and headed home, preparing for this evening's Cub Scout den meeting. I had to admit, deep down inside, I was thinking this might be a good thing. I was holding out hope that I would fit in and make new friends. My mom walked me to the house, rang the bell, handed me off to the den leader, and disappeared into the night. I was scared. I was nervous. I was ready. As we headed up the stairs and into the living room, there were ten to twelve boys sitting in a circle. I looked on in horror as I noticed they were wearing the same uniforms—dark-blue shirts, blazers, and pants with yellow sashes and scarves held in place nicely with cool-looking metal Boy Scout sleeves. These were a far cry from the drab green shirt and flood pants (no sash, no scarf) I was wearing. Let's not forget, I was wearing my Sunday choir shoes (shiny black patent) while all the other boys had on their cool gym shoes. My face turned red. Tears streamed down my cheek as I was led to my place in the circle. As boys will be boys, even at that young age, they rode me mercilessly. The rest of the night was a blur; I could not remember much else, which was a good thing. The one thing I do remember is being assigned our first task as a Boy Scout. We would be working on our woodworking badge. We were all told to go home, come up with a project, work with our fathers to design and build it, and come prepared to present at next week's meeting. A chance to spend time with my dad. A real bonding moment. Seeing he was an architect, this project should be a slam dunk. I couldn't wait to show my tormentors what I had created.

I went home and told my father. He appeared indifferent; maybe he'd had a long day. No big deal. Days went by without a word from my father. It was now midweek, and we had not started our project.

"Please, Dad, we need to get started."

"I'm up to my ears right now, Bob. We'll get to it shortly."

A few more days went by and nothing. It was now Friday night, less than twenty-four hours from my next meeting. I was in panic mode. How the hell were we going to get this done in time? My dad was sleeping on the couch in front of the TV. He was not going anywhere. I guess I was on my own. I headed to the basement. Reminder, I was in third grade and knew absolutely jack shit about designing or building anything. I had never even touched a tool. *What the hell am I going to make? I got it, why not build an airplane?* I picked up two pieces of wood (unfinished, mind you). I grabbed a nail (looking back, it was probably a five-inch commercial nail) and hammer. I proceeded to do the best I could to nail the two pieces of wood together. After more than thirty minutes of finger-breaking effort, I had the nail all the way through. I then proceeded to bang on the piece of the nail that was extruding from the bottom until it was folded back against the wood. What next? I had to make it look more like a plane than a cross. I got out my watercolors and markers. I spent the next several hours decorating my plane. I painted the entire unit yellow (several times, as the watercolors soaked into the wood) and drew in the details (windows, people, whatever) with a black marker. It was done. Who needed Dad? I was so excited by the masterpiece I had created. I couldn't wait to show my fellow Cub Scouts.

Twenty-four hours later, and it was time to head off to my meeting. My dad was nowhere to be found. I grabbed my plane and headed out the door, smiling from ear to ear. As I headed into the den mother's living room, my joy once again turned to excruciating pain. Spread out on the floor were beautiful bookshelves, birdhouses, rocking chairs, etc. All were finished in lacquer or brightly painted. As I assumed my position in the circle, I thought I was going to puke. It was time for each boy to describe their project, sharing all the details leading up to its completion. I had my plane hidden under my shirt. *What the hell am I going to do?* It was my turn. I pulled my plane out, tears running down my eyes. I could barely put a sentence together as the other boys laughed and screamed at me. Somehow, I got through it. The meeting was now over, and I wanted nothing more than to get home and hide in my room. I was never coming out again! As I headed for the door, the den mother, with tears in her eyes, handed me a brightly colored woodworking badge. She felt so bad for me she gave me one even though I failed miserably on my attempt. Kids may be brutal to other kids, but at least there are a few good adults in this world.

Next on the docket was the biggest Cub Scout event of the year. It was what they called the pinewood derby, scheduled for early December. A downhill racetrack would be set up in the church hall. Each of the Scouts had the next several months to build a car with their father in preparation for racing one another until a winner was crowned. This was open not only to my den but also to *all* Scouts in the parish. There would be several hundred participants. This was the big one! I took my instruction booklet home and gave it to my father. I told him how important this was to me. Working with my dad to design and build the fastest and coolest-looking car would most certainly make up for my wood badge fiasco. I'd stay on his ass until this was done. No excuses. September went by. Then October. Fast-forward to Thanksgiving. Nothing but excuses to this point. I was begging him on a daily basis. We were a week away from the event, and again, nothing. I guess I'd get started, and he could jump in.

I was back into the basement. I found a block of wood. I needed to "carve" it down into the shape of a race car. I grabbed a fifteen-inch handsaw and went at it. I had no idea what the hell I was doing. I hacked away for hours until there was a slight curve in the block. Close enough. Wheels? I broke off two sets of axles and wheels from one of my remaining (smaller) Tonka trucks. I found an industrial-type stapler in my dad's tools and proceeded to "staple" the axles to the bottom of the woodblock. Some more watercolors and markers and I was good to go. I kept the car out of sight until the day arrived. This was a father-son event. As we neared departure time, my father told my mother that he was tired and wouldn't be able to attend. After a few minutes of back-and-forth, my father assumed his position on the couch, and my mother and I headed over to the church hall.

Kids were flying around everywhere. There was a huge track in the center of the hall. Not one mother in sight. I awkwardly sat down in the corner of the room, awaiting my turn to race my car. As I looked around, I could see, once again, I had been severely outclassed when it came to my car. Theirs had sleek bodies, beautiful paint jobs, chrome wheels. I saw where this one was going.

"Sorensen, Johnson, please step to the track!"

I was crying even before my butt lifted from the seat. I took my block of wood to the starting gate. People, including adults this time, were laughing and talking. I was so embarrassed I wanted to melt into the floor. As Mark Johnson placed his miniature Indy-style car next to my "doorstop", he knew it was over before it started. The gate was lifted, and his car screamed down the track. My car? It went about six feet before the staple on the front axle broke off, and my car froze in place. My evening came to a screeching halt. I took my piece of shit back to my seat. My mom told me, "You can't win them all." I demanded to leave immediately. I'd seen enough. I'd been through enough embarrassment for one night. I just wanted to go back to my cell.

*****

Let's stay in the same month and year to give you some brief insight into Christmas at the Sorensen house. Like any other child, I would spend several months putting my wish list together for Santa. We were always told that if you were a good boy or girl, Santa would be good to you. By this time (third grade), I was hearing stories about Santa not being real. In actuality, your parents were the ones providing the gifts. I tried not to listen, but in reality, I didn't care. As long as I get what I want, I'm a happy camper. I carefully made up my list. Like they said, I checked it twice. I gave it to my parents to forward to Santa well in advance of Christmas Day. Better safe than sorry.

It was now Christmas Eve. We put out cookies and milk for Santa and his reindeers and ran off to bed. I had a hard time falling asleep because my mind was working overtime (more than usual). After many hours of tossing and turning, I was back awake. It was 6:00 a.m., and I was raring to go. I woke up my oldest sister, and we headed down. The tree was all lit up, with presents surrounding the base. We looked for each of our piles and began to touch, feel, shake, etc., trying to get a hint of what was inside. We were going to bust. We tore down to my parents' bedroom and swan dove into their bed.

"Wake Up! Santa came!"

My parents hemmed and hawed. They told us it was too early and to go back to bed.

"Are you crazy? Didn't you hear me? Santa came, and I'm ready to tear into those presents while I go down my checklist."

They lay motionless. We headed back to the tree and proceeded to wait another forty-five-plus minutes until they wandered into the living room. Instead of letting us go crazy, my parents had this tradition of only opening one present at a time in order from oldest to youngest. Karen, followed by me, followed by my youngest sister, Laura. It was time to begin, and I was about to pee my pants with excitement. Present 1, Christmas stocking cap and scarf. Present 2, a pair of polka dot mittens (that's correct, mittens, not gloves). Present 3, a robe. Present 4, underwear. This went on and on throughout the morning. We were getting down to the last few presents. I was still holding out hope I'd get something, anything, off my list. Next present, a hard cover copy of the Children's Bible. Last present, some obscure board game. It appeared another Christmas had come and gone, and Santa (or my parents) had stiffed me once again! My face went flush. I began to cry uncontrollably. My parents had just taken the happiest day in a kid's life and made it the worst day. I was told not to cry, that Santa brought me everything that I "needed." It was not about needed! This was the kind of shit you should be buying for your children all along, not saving it up to disguise as Christmas gift. I was devastated. Insult to injury was when you return to school after the break just to hear about all the cool things my fellow classmates received. Brutal. Unfortunately, this would be how Christmas would go every year, far into my teenage years.

*****

It was now the summer of 1971. I had managed to make a few more friends at school. Our interests had now turned to sports. Summer, baseball. Fall, football. Winter, hockey. Spring, basketball. There was no such thing as organized sports back then. You just pulled together the kids in the neighborhood, split up the sides, and played. It was baseball season, and everyone was ready to go. Seeing Santa was good to my friends over the years, they all had the required gear—gloves, bats, hats, etc. Me? I had several pairs of beautiful mittens, forty pairs of underwear, etc. No sports gear of any kind. Seeing I had zero dollars to my name (*all* birthday and Christmas money I may have gotten is in the bank, there was no such thing as an allowance), I had to ask my mom to please buy me what I needed.

"That's a boy thing. Go ask your dad."

"Not Dad! Please, not Dad!"

Let me remind you of two things. My father was a momma's boy who never played a sport in his life. My father spent zero time with me because he was always too "busy" with work and other activities (from early childhood on, my dad's favorite pastime was lying on the couch). I asked anyways, and for the next several weeks, I got the standard runaround. My mother picked up on this and decided to take matters into her own hands. Back to Goldblatt's we go. I didn't know jack shit about sporting gear. My mom knew even less. As a result, we let price determine our decision.

"What's the difference? They all do the same thing."

We picked out a shiny plastic baseball glove, barely larger than my Christmas mittens, and a Cubs hat, most certainly not the official MLB gear. The brim came to a point like a bird's beak. The *C* was grossly oversized and the wrong color (purple). We headed home. I put on a pair of flannel pants, a button-down mini-me polo shirt, and my play shoes (Buster Brown loafers). I grabbed my mitt and hat and bolted out the front door to the park. I was so excited I could bust. Upon my arrival, I could see I was most definitely over dressed for the occasion. Of course, everyone was in T-shirts, blue jeans, and gym shoes. After getting my ass handed to me for the next fifteen to twenty minutes (verbally), we finally got around to picking teams. Mind you, I've never played a second of baseball in my life. The only exposure I've had was watching the Cubs play on WGN-TV. I was told to play third base. I assumed my position. Play ball. The first kid up hit a soft line drive my way. I put my glove up in front of my face in an attempt to catch the ball. The good news was, I was able to catch the ball in my mitt. The bad news was, the ball proceeded to rip through my plastic glove and nail me straight in the eye. The first play of my baseball career and I was not only injured but also my mitt was destroyed. Of course, I was crying like a little schoolgirl. The other kids were laughing their asses off while I sprinted back to my house.

My mother greeted me at the door. "What's wrong?" I relayed my story as she put ice on my eye. She told me to be a big boy and stop crying. I just got hit straight in my eye with a baseball because of the piece of shit glove she bought me and she wanted me to be a big boy? So much for sympathy from your mother. As I held the ice pack on my eye, my mother went in the other room to track down a shoelace. She took my mangled glove, put it back together with the lace, handed it back to me, and said, "See, good as new. Now get back out there and have some fun."

Man, I just couldn't win. I did as I was told. I headed back over. I took my lumps. Midway through the summer, one of my friends gave me a spare glove that he had. I don't remember who that was. Whoever you were, I love you, man! Fall came, and it was the same story. Back to Goldblatt's for a Kansas City Chiefs helmet with no padding. Of course, it was on sale. I wore it once, got my ass kicked, and threw it into my closet, never to be seen again. From this point on, I would play full-contact football with no helmet or pads.

Winter brought hockey season, along with a pair of figure skates and an off-brand hockey stick. I refused to *ever* wear the skates. I chose to play ice hockey in my boots. The stick broke within thirty minutes of use (of course), and I had to rely on the generosity of others once again. I chose to skip basketball entirely because my parents bought me an undersized rubber ball, and I had yet to get a pair of gym shoes. My sports career was off and running.

*****

This is a perfect time to talk about music. Music was a very important thing in the Sorensen house, as long as you were listening to the "appropriate" type of music. My mom was absolutely nuts about jazz—any and all types of jazz. My father was into the big band sound. There was not a day that would go by without either playing on the family turntable. Karen was starting to branch out into the pop music of the day—Helen Reddy, the Carpenters, Herb Alpert. All the above were deemed appropriate and acceptable. Not knowing any better, I accepted this as the norm. At the time, we did not have a radio, so there was no exposure to other types of music that was out there. My parents loved jazz and big band music. My sister liked pop music. I, by default, loved it all. As you can imagine, when this subject came up amongst my friends, I once again fell victim to more physical and verbal abuse. To summarize, I was heading into fourth grade, and I was this skinny, dorky, effeminate, brainwashed little boy. No true father figure. Raised by a mother who knew nothing about raising a boy, choosing to raise (and dress) me like another daughter. To be blunt, I was fucked at this point. I was trapped, and there was no way out. God help me.

*****

The fall of 1971 saw me entering into the fourth grade. A new year meant a new pair of Buddy Holly glasses. At this point, I refused to wear them in school. God knows I'm getting my ass ripped for other issues. I don't want to give my tormentors anything else to zero in on. The problem was, I couldn't see the board without them. I didn't care. I was more worried about survival than I was about my performance in school. Of course, my grades began to suffer. Sister Alodia, my teacher at the time, was sending progress reports home with me for my parents. My parents were supposed to read her comments, sign off, and return with me to school. I knew once my parents saw these reports, I was a dead man. What can I do to circumvent? Now I have to give myself credit for creativity on this one. Hear me out. As I mentioned earlier, my father was an architect. He had velum (tracing) paper in his basement office. I grabbed a piece of that paper, along with a canceled check from the bank (not sure how I tracked that down), and headed up to my room. I laid the paper over my mother's signature on the check and traced it onto velum. Once that was complete, I took the tracing paper and laid it over the signature area on the progress report. With a ballpoint pen, I pushed down hard on the signature until I was complete. This made a perfect indention on the progress report. I would then remove the tracing paper and fill in the indented area with my pen. Perfect match! I brought it back the next day, and not a word was said. This went on every week until mid-November, during parent-teacher conference time.

We headed on over to the school, my parents totally oblivious of what had been happening over the last several months. We sat down, and Sister Alodia dropped the bomb. "Robert is doing terrible in all his classes. You must take a more active role in his studies. In addition, we think his eyes should be tested. He may need glasses. He appears to be having trouble seeing the board, even from the front row." (I wonder how I ended up there.)

My parents were shocked and quite pissed off. "Why is this the first we are hearing about this?"

Surprised, Sister Alodia pulled out the stack of signed-off progress reports and handed them to my parents. Busted! My parents told my teacher they had never seen these and that all had been forged. They also informed her that I'd worn glasses since I was a child. A few more pleasantries were exchanged, along with many an apology. We headed home in silence. After a ten-minute spanking session and thirty-minute verbal abuse session, I was sent to my room, the eye hook attached. Other than school and meals, that was where I would stay for the next two weeks. No crying jag, no head banging was going to get you out of this one.

*****

At this point, I need to digress a bit. Over the past summer, I met a new friend in the neighborhood. His name was Stevie. He was a year younger than me, lived five houses to the west of mine, and attended the local public school. He was so different from my other friends. He was nonjudgmental of my appearance, behavior, or tendencies. He, for whatever reason, accepted me for who I was. He was the coolest kid I had ever met in my short life. Little did I know at this point just how much of an impact Stevie would have on my life!

The Transition

It was the end of fourth grade, and somehow, some way, I had passed all my classes by the skin of my teeth. I was now counting down the minutes before we could run out that front door and start our summer vacation. It was the summer of 1972. *Ring.* I was out like a shot. I changed into my play clothes and headed straight down to the house of my newfound friend, Stevie. As mentioned, he was, by far, the coolest kid I have met in my short lifetime. In addition to doing all the things boys do at this stage in my life (bike riding, playing pinners off the garage door, playing tag, etc.), he had turned me onto other more interesting activities. We would catch bugs and throw them into spider webs. We would watch the spiders attack and kill the bugs. When that was completed, we would take out a magnifying glass and, with the help of the rays of the sun, burn the whole damn thing down. We would catch fireflies, remove the lights from their tails, and make jewelry out of them (rings, necklaces, etc.). They would glow for hours in the dark! He had access to fireworks, which opened up a whole new world to us. There was nothing we wouldn't blow up.

Our favorite pastime was digging trenches in his backyard, strategically placing plastic army men throughout and lobbing fire-crackers (like grenades) at them. Sometimes we would just cut to the chase by taping the explosive to the army guy and just blowing the shit out of them. We would do this for hours each day. This took my earlier destructive behavior to a whole new level, and I loved it! Don't ask me where the adult supervision was. At his house, nothing was off-limits. We were free to use our imagination to come up with any and all off-the-chart activities. My world changed forever once I was allowed into his house. He lived in a three-story bungalow, similar to my house with a slight twist. His grandparents resided on the first floor. His single aunt lived in the attic (where my room at home was). His family lived in the basement.

One would think the basement would be refurbished to make it more like a home environment. This was not the case. As you made your way down the concrete steps in the back of the house, you entered through an aluminum storm door. This was the only entrance to their living area. As you walked in, there was a small dark room immediately to the right. It couldn't have been more than ten feet by ten feet. A few feet beyond that was a small washroom with very rudimentary plumbing fixtures (small toilet, bathtub, etc.). Moving forward, you would reach an accordion door. Open that door, and you had gone into a kitchen, living, and bedroom area. A stove and refrigerator to the right. A TV and couch in the center, and two rollout beds at the far-left side of the room. Stevie's bed was against the wall with a three-foot separation from his parents' bed. Head back out through the accordion doors, into the center of the home. It was completely open in the center, with the exception of a flight of stairs leading up to the first floor of the house. On the right side of that open area, you would find a washer and dryer, with a table full of electronic gear of all kinds, lit up like a Christmas tree. It turned out to be a ham radio setup. Stevie's father was into ham radio operation big-time. He would spend hours at that command center talking to people all over the world. As a kid, I thought it was the coolest thing in the world. In fact, I thought the Stevie's house was the coolest place to live that I have ever seen. Little did I know it would get even better.

That first room on the right, as you walk through the front door, was the bedroom of Stevie's older brothers—Ricky, three years older than Stevie, and Gary, the oldest, two years older than Ricky. The front of their doorway was covered, floor to ceiling, with dark glass beads. As you push back the beads and enter the room, there was absolutely no light or color of any kind. They had covered every inch of the walls with what appeared to be black wallpaper of some kind. The window was also painted over in black. The right side of the room contained bunk beds covered in dark-purple sheets and bedspreads. I'd never seen bunk beds and could not believe how cool they were. On the left side of the bedroom, there were two overstuffed beanbag chairs (of course, black in color). Up against the center wall was a short table housing a unit similar to the ham radio setup. Knobs, dials, screens, etc. all glowing in a dark-blue hue. On both sides of the table rest two wooden cabinets, three to four feet in height, with black circles cut out of all different diameters. There was what appeared to be a small vase on one of the cabinets. Something sweet-smelling was smothering in that vase. In the light sockets (two) were purple light bulbs, providing an eerie glow over the entire room. I would find out through an endless series of questions what all this stuff were—a stereo, a turntable, black lights, incense.

The whole room, the whole scene was beyond comprehension for my young mind to process. All I knew was, it was the coolest room I had ever seen! It would get even better. As I was sitting on one of the beanbag chairs, I was listening to the music coming out of the stereo speakers. I'd never heard music like this in my entire life. It was loud. It was fast. It was electrifying. Mind you, up until this point, I've been listening to all the crap music my parents deemed as acceptable—jazz, big band, pop. This was *nothing* like that. I was drawn into this music like a moth to a flame. The more I hear, the more I want! I could not get enough of it. I sat for hours listening to record after record. I had found religion! This was the turning point in my short life, and I knew it! I was so emotional I began to tear up. Thank God it was dark in the room, so no one could see me crying.

Black Sabbath.

Deep Purple.

Led Zeppelin.

Uriah Heep.

Cream.

The list went on and on. I stayed until the brothers kicked me out of the room. I headed home a different person. I'd found Jesus! I'd seen the light! My heart was pounding. My head was spinning. Nothing would ever be the same. I settled into a pattern. I would wake up and head down to Stevie's house immediately. We would spend the morning killing bugs, digging trenches, and blowing things up. We would spend the afternoon (the brothers generally sleep in until noon) hanging out in his brothers' room, breathing in all flavors of incense while listening to heavy metal music of all kinds. I was in heaven! How could life get any better?

*****

After several weeks of this routine, I decided it was time for me to get my first heavy metal album. I gathered up what little money I had. Stevie and I headed down to Goldblatt's record department. After much deliberation, I settled on my purchase—Burn by Deep Purple. What a cool album cover (the faces of the band in the form of burning candles). Great songs (I've heard it numerous times in the brothers' room). I completed my transaction and headed home. Earlier in the year, my parents gave me a record player, with a built-in speaker, to listen to my sister's Carpenters 45s. I changed the setting on the player, loaded my record, and turned the knob all the way to the right. The record began, and I once again found myself shedding tears of joy. Granted, the sound quality was poor compared to the brothers' stereo. I didn't care. It was my record. It was the sound of Deep Purple reverberating off my bedroom walls. I was on my way.

Of course, my parents came upstairs to see what the "noise" was all about. They heard the music, saw the album cover, saw the smile on my face, and immediately went nuts.

"What have you done?"

"What is this garbage you are listening to?"

"This is how you spend what little money that you have?"

I was devastated.

"Don't you see? Can't you hear it? This is like religion to me!"

My mother turned off the player, removed the record, put it in its sleeve, and demanded me to take it back to the store. I went nuts. I began screaming, yelling, kicking, etc., anything to make her go away and be quiet. She stormed out of the room, slammed the door, and fastened the eye hook. What she didn't understand was that I'd won. See if I give a shit if you lock me into my room. I've got my record player; I've got my album. I turned it back on, lowered the volume, and listened to the record over and over again. As I listened, I explored the album cover and sleeve. By the time I was done, I knew every inch of that album and every word of every song. It was emblazoned in my brain. You could never take that away from me!

As I mentioned earlier, discovering this music was life-altering. It was hard. It was fast. It was energizing. It truly was an expression of me—how my mind worked, how I felt. Knowing there were others in the world listening to this music, sharing the same thoughts and feeling that I did, gave me the strength and confidence I had been missing up until this point in my life. My self-confidence was off the charts! First order of business was to go back and take care of all my tormentors. By this time, I had grown a few inches and put on a few pounds. Most of the bullies I was dealing with were younger and smaller than me. The main reason they were able to kick my ass was because I was told not to fight back but to reason with them. That, along with no confidence and low self-esteem, made me an easy target. Not any longer! The time for reasoning was over! I was now on a mission. One by one, I sought out my tormenters, starting with Billy. I was at the park when he approached me. As anticipated, he started right in, calling me names, poking me in the chest. I didn't know how to fight but had a rough idea how to inflict some pain. I grabbed that little son of a bitch, put him in a headlock, and began to rain punches down onto his head. I didn't really know how to throw a proper punch. I just closed my fist and pounded on the top of his head until he hit the ground. I got on top of him and continued doing the same across his back and neck. He was crying like a little girl, begging me to get off him. Eventually, he was able to break clear and run home to his mommy. One by one, I did the same to each of my tormentors. The message was sent loud and clear. I was no longer anyone's punching bag. I was nobody to fuck with. Thank you, Black Sabbath, for giving me the courage to stand up for myself.

*****

Next on my agenda was to quit the all-girls choir. I'm not a girl; I'm a boy. I needed to put a stop to this immediately. I went to the church rectory to speak with the pastor and inform him of my decision. He was not pleased. He asked me if my parents were aware of my decision. I lied. "They most certainly are." I knew lying to a priest was a sin. I didn't give a shit. I wanted out and didn't care. My mind-set at the time was I'd rather be happy and go to hell than to live in misery and go to heaven. When Sunday came around and I did not go to church to sing in the choir, my parents asked what was going on. I told them I had quit earlier in the week. They were pissed. They once again sent me to my room and locked me in.

"You sit in there and think about what you did wrong!"

No problem. I put my record on and listened to it, over and over again, for the next several hours. Punishment my ass. Thank you, Deep Purple.

*****

Back in the days, there was no such thing as an allowance. You were expected to do a series of daily/weekly chores with no payment. Period. That said, we were always poor as kids. As mentioned earlier, any birthday money you may have received went directly into your bank account.

"You need to save for the future."

I bought my first album with the few coins I had lying around. I was out of money. As I continued to hang at Stevie's and listen to more and more tunes with his brothers, I wanted to start building up my record collection. Very tough to do with no cash. Once a week (every Wednesday), we would get a small paper delivered to our house. It was called the *Leader*. It was a local newspaper, covering all the happenings in the neighborhood. I would read it religiously as a large percentage of the stories were covering grade and high school sporting events (sports was rapidly becoming my second love and passion in this world, a close second to music). One day, while reading the paper, I noticed an ad looking for paperboys—someone to deliver the *Leader* in the neighborhood. Deliver once a week. Collect the money owed once a month. Make money. Outstanding! Sounds simple enough. I can do that. I would then have plenty of money to buy more music.

I immediately rushed down to the *Leader* newspaper office and signed up. I would start next week. The following Wednesday, a stack of papers and a bag of rubber bands were dropped off on my front porch, along with a map of my route. I hurriedly rolled the papers and loaded them in to my granny cart (wire mesh box with two wheels and a handle). I went door to door slinging the *Leader* newspaper onto each of my neighbor's front porches. Simple enough. At month's end, I was given a roll of tickets and a vinyl bag. I went door to door collecting the fees owed for the paper. To my surprise, not only did you collect the fee but you also received what they called tips—money given by people, out of the goodness of their hearts, for you doing a good job of delivery. I got paid a certain percentage for each house I collected from along with 100 percent of my tip money. Within several months, I was rich (from a kid's perspective)! As my stack of cash grew, so did my album collection. By the end of the summer, my collection went from one record up to a dozen. I was on my way! I learned several lessons from an early age. First off, if you really want something, you have to go after it with all your heart and soul. Second, you control your own destiny. Third, and most importantly, money *can* buy you happiness (especially when you're a kid).

*****

As mentioned earlier, along with music, sports began playing a much bigger role in my life. As I look back, that summer of 1972 was one of the most memorable in my fifty-seven years on this planet. By this point, the fifth-grade sports clique was fully developed, and I was a big part of it. Just like the movie *The Sandlot*, each of us had an established position to play—George, third base; Rick, short stop; Joe, second base; Chris, first base; Adam, right field; Dominic, center field; Michael, pitcher; Gerry, catcher. Me? I played left field. Seeing most of our players were right-handed, the left side of the field had some of the most important positions—left field being the most critical. I had elevated my status by playing baseball all the time. I would play catch with my friends for hours. I would throw pop-ups to myself every day. In between, I would play pinners off the front steps of my house. The most important activity? I would stand in left field, throw pop-ups to myself, and practice throwing the baseball, on a line, to each of the bases (home plate being the most concentrated on). Catch. Throw. Retrieve. Repeat. Hour after hour. By the end of the day, my arm was so sore I could barely pick up a fork to eat dinner.

In the early days, they called this "throwing your arm out." Supposedly, the more you did this, the stronger your arm became. Sounds good to me. A regular day would begin at 8:00 a.m. in Chopin Park. We would gather at the diamond across the street from my house and practice our positions for several hours. After that, we would break up into teams (never enough to cover all positions on each team, so we would deem several areas as out-of-bounds) and play two to three nine inning games. After that was complete, we would head home for the day, where we would all pick up on our daily drills (as outlined above). By midsummer, we were a well-oiled machine. We were fast. We were athletic. Our coordination was outstanding. We were confident and cocky little shits.

One day in mid to late July, we ran into a group of older boys playing on the diamond kiddie corner from our usual spot. We paid them no mind. We set up shop and began going through our usual routine. Not even five minutes in, these guys started giving us a bunch of shit. They turned out to be the sixth-grade boys from St. Ladislaus (one year ahead of us). They were deliberately running onto our field, stealing our ball, calling us names, etc. After thirty minutes of back-and-forth, one of my big-mouth teammates told them, "Shut the fuck up and leave us alone!" All eighteen kids on the field froze for a second. In a blink of an eye, the older kids were on our diamond, ready to square off. This was it. I was going to die. Just then, the "reasoning" skills my parents taught me at an early age kicked in. I rushed to the mound where the leader of their pack was screaming at Mike.

I said, "Instead of fighting, why don't we play a game against each other to see who the better of the two teams are?"

Their leader laughed in my face. He went onto say, "There's no way in hell you guys will ever beat us. You're on!"

The party broke up, and the sixth-grade boys headed back to their field. At first, everyone on my team wanted to kick my ass for opening my mouth. However, as we talked it through, everyone began to get excited.

"We're just as good as them!"

"Do you know what it would mean to beat the sixth-grade boys?"

We immediately assumed our positions and began to practice like we'd never practiced before. No more two hours here, two hours there. We were now practicing and playing from sunup to sundown. The game had been set for the end of next week, and we were going to be ready!

On the day of the game, we headed over to the park house. Back then, you could borrow equipment from them for any sport. We grabbed all four bases, a pitching rubber, and full catcher's gear.

We headed out to the field and set this baby up like it was Wrigley Field. Each team took about fifteen minutes to warm up prior to the game. We were ready. They were ready. Let's go. We played a full nine inning game. The score went back and forth. Tons of cheating on both sides (we called our own balls and strikes, along with safe/out calls at each base). It was a hell of a game, but unfortunately, we came out on the losing side, 19–17. The sixth graders strutted around like peacocks. Several of us were on the verge of tears. We certainly had nothing to be ashamed of.

"We'll be back, and when we do, we're going to kick your ass!"

Little did we know that this would be a rivalry that would last through the balance of our grade school years. Not only baseball. Football—both one-hundred-yard tackle, without pads, as well as intramural. Hockey—both ice (frozen pond at Chopin Park) as well as intramural (playing on the asphalt parking lot at St. Ladislaus). I was very proud to say we won many a game against our rivals! Our strong attribute? We were fearless. We would sacrifice our bodies to make a play—slide on the asphalt, in our corduroy pants, to block a puck; slam our head into the chest of our opponent to prevent them from gaining another yard on the gridiron. There was nothing we wouldn't do to beat these SOBs. Looking back, I am so proud of my class/teammates. We sure as hell showed them!

*****

A big part of being a kid at this point was to show just how tough you are in front of others. For whatever reason, I decided the best way to do this was to begin cursing like a sailor. I certainly picked up a few words from my parents over the years. Nothing too earth-shattering but certainly my baseline. *God*, *damn*, *crap*, *shit*—all made their way into my daily vocabulary. Any chance I would get, outside my home, of course, to add these into my conversations (outbursts), I would take full advantage of it. At this point, I was still spending a ton of time with Stevie's older brothers. They introduced me to the next series of curse words. The down and dirty stuff—*fuck*, *cunt*, *jag off*. You get the picture. All these words sounded cool. All these words sounded tough. In my mind, saying these words made you an adult. I was off and running. Of course, being the age that I was, I had no idea what any of these words meant. I would soon find out the damage that could be done when using one of the "top tier" words in the wrong setting.

My family took a trip down to the home of my Grandma Gabrick (my mother's mother) in Central Illinois. Of course, I didn't want to be there. I wanted to be home, playing with my friends. Of course, I was pouting, whining like a big baby, making everyone's life miserable. I was sitting in a rocking chair in my grandma's living room. My whining continued.

My mother said, "It's a beautiful day. Stop your whining and go outside."

This made me even more pissed. I wanted to inflict some damage. I turned around to face my mother (my father and grandma are in the background) and screamed out, "Shut the fuck up, you cock sucker!"

The room went silent for a second. My father's face was beet red, his eyes spinning in his head like pinwheels. He proceeded to charge the rocking chair, hitting it with full force with me still in it. He threw the chair aside and pinned me on my stomach. He started raining down blows, one after another, to all parts of my body. This went on for about five minutes. I was crying. I was screaming "I'm sorry!" Nothing seemed to faze him. He finally seemed to be running out of steam. Thank God. He got up right about the time my mom assumed the same position. Now she was raining down blows. *Bing! Bang! Boom!* I happened to catch a glance of my grandma out of the corner of my eye. Was she cheering them on? Wasn't this the time she was supposed to be stepping in to save me? No help came. After what seemed like an hour, the beatdown came to an end. I was sore as hell. My voice was shot from all the screaming I'd done. Note to self: *never ever*, *ever* use a curse word in front of your family, especially your mother. Whatever *fuck* and *cock sucker* meant, it must be bad/ nasty. Good shit to use on your classmates in the schoolyard.

*****

Over the next several years, I would continue to spend as much time as I could with Ricky and Gary, soaking up their music like a sponge. By this point, I had discovered the next wave of heavy metal music.

Judas Priest.

Iron Maiden.

Scorpions.

Thin Lizzy.

Aerosmith.

UFO.

Humble Pie.

Heavier. Louder. Faster. I loved it! I couldn't get enough of it. My album collection continued to grow. I spent every penny I earned on music. I'd even branched out to purchasing music paraphernalia. Posters to decorate my room. Pins and patches to wear on my jackets. I was one cool son of a bitch (so I thought)! About this time, I was introduced to a band called Kiss. When I first saw them, I thought they were the greatest thing I had ever seen. When I heard them, I was even more hooked. Then came the Kiss Army Fan Club. For $10, you would get a Kiss poster, patch, membership card, and *dog tags*! I was in! I bought every album they had put out to date. I put them into my listening rotation and added them to both phase 1 and 2 of my existing collection, and I was happier than a pig in shit. Of course, my parents weren't too happy. They believed all the music I was listening to was satanic in nature.

"We raised our son to be Catholic, and he's turning into a devil worshipper."

I don't care. Let them think that. This music has defined my life. It's given me a purpose. You will never ever take that away from me. Period.

*****

Let's talk about fire for a minute. About this time, my friends and I had discovered fire. It started out small. We would light a piece of paper in the alley and watch it burn. We would find an anthill and light it up. Simple things. We were mesmerized by the flames, the damage it could inflict. After listening to tunes, followed by a full day of sports, we would turn to fire for some additional jollies. There are three stories in particular that come to mind during this period. Each story shows the elevation of its importance in our young minds.

The summer of 1974, we just finished up playing some baseball. At the time, we used pieces of cardboard as bases. Instead of just taking that cardboard and discarding it, someone had the bright idea to pile it all against the backstop and set it on fire. One problem: the backstop was made of wood. We lit it up and watched it smother. All at once it lit up. The flames were getting stronger and higher. The wooden backstop was immediately on fire. It was out of control. Everyone scattered. I, along with several of my friends, headed to my house. We shot up into my bedroom. My window had a clear view of the park. We all jammed our heads against the screen to watch the bonfire we created, as we listened to the fire engine sirens wailing in the distance. The fire department arrived and doused the flames. We smiled as the black smoke filled the air.

Several weeks later, we were in the alley behind Mike Bialas's house. We had located an empty shopping cart and had come up with a brilliant idea.

"Let's stuff the cart full of paper, cardboard, etc., then light it on fire and push it around a bit. A mobile bonfire!"

We completed the task, and away we went. *Poof!* Flames were immediately shooting several feet in the air. We panicked. We pushed the cart into a telephone pole. The flames were now licking the pole and melting the electric lines. Once again, we scattered. Hiding in a friend's backyard, we once again heard the sirens in the background and awaited the fire department's arrival. As they put out the fire, we celebrated our success.

This last story was totally out of control but must be told. We got creative. After watching army movies on TV, we got the bright idea to make our own homemade gas bombs. We gathered up ten to fifteen glass baby food jars. We filled each with an ounce or two of gasoline. We put a piece of rag in each and screwed the top down, leaving a portion of the rag to hang on the outside. (Note: we have never seen or heard of a Molotov cocktail.) We went down to an empty lot on Diversey and Central (major intersection in Chicago). There were six of us. Three went to one side of the lot; the other three went to the other side. We proceeded to light our jars on fire and throw them at one another. It was exactly like the war scenes on TV. As the jars hit the ground, the gasoline lit up, and flames were shooting everywhere. We were laughing our asses off as the carnage continued. Cars stopped in the middle of the street. People could not believe what they were seeing. Finally, a police officer showed up at the scene. We once again scattered. I ran the entire eight blocks home and bolted up to my bedroom. I smelled of gasoline. I had black smudge marks on my arms. I was smiling from ear to ear. That was the coolest thing I had ever seen! I was that far gone.

*****

This seems like the appropriate time to talk about sex. We were familiar with the word. We laughed every time someone used the word. We acted like we knew what it was. In actuality, we had no clue. I was curious as hell but was afraid to ask anyone about it because they would think I was a dork and make fun of me. I tried to pick up as much as I could from others' conversations, but I was still in the dark. I had several "encounters" over the next several years that lead to even more confusion. Let me share them with you in the order they took place.

I was in my left field position one sunny afternoon. It was a day like any other day. My eyes were scanning the horizon when I zoned in on a couple sitting off to the right of my position. They were on a blanket, under the shade of a tree. They were locked at the lips, hands surveying each other's bodies. This went on for quite some time. At this point, the young man slipped out of his pants, his penis exposed for all the world to see. The young lady put her hand on his penis and began to stroke it. The more she stroked, the larger it got. At that moment, I thought about my own little boy penis and could not comprehend what the hell was going on. Was he sick? As if it couldn't get any worse, the young lady put his penis in her mouth and proceeded to go up and down on it. Fucking gross! The boy appeared to be writhing in pain. Was she biting it off? Just what in the hell was going on? After what seemed like a few hours, the girl stopped, and both rolled over in a heap of arms and legs. He was smiling and laughing. He most certainly was not in any pain.

In between innings, I shared my story with my other teammates. Their eyes were like pinwheels. First, they said I was lying.

Then they called me stupid. One of my friends said, "Don't you know anything? She was giving him a blow job."

"What the hell is that?"

Of course, he had no idea other than what it was called. I was left to my own imagination. I went home that evening and examined my own penis. It was very small compared to the one I saw earlier. Try as I may, I could not make it get any bigger. Then I came up with my own conclusions on what a blow job was. She was either blowing into the small hole at the end of the penis, or he was, for whatever reason, peeing in her mouth. What else was a penis used for? I patted myself on the back. I figured it out all on my own. What a smart little shit I was.

The next two situations happened while I was at two different swimming locations. The first was on a water slide at Wonder Lake (my uncle took us there every summer). These were not the water slides of today. This was an all-metal slide positioned several feet out into the water. Everyone went up the metal steps, slid down, and got back in line. I was four or five steps up the ladder when a mother in front of me playfully yelled at her daughter to "keep moving." As she did that, she yanked on her daughter's bathing suit bottom and proceeded (accidentally) to pull them down to her ankles. I was now staring straight up at a young girl's bottom/private part. I couldn't stop staring because I had never seen the opposite sex naked at any time in my short life. The poor girl was mortified. The mother helped her pull them back up as quickly as she could. I couldn't stop thinking about what I saw. So different from my own body. The same thing happened a few months later. I was visiting my grandma's house in Central Illinois, and we decided to head over to the local pool with our cousins. Upon arrival, we decided to play water tag. I was *it* to start with because I was the youngest of the bunch. Five or so minutes into the game, I was swimming underwater, attempting to tag my cousin Julie. I was underwater, eyes open, swimming like a wild man as I reached out to tag her. I inadvertently grabbed her suit bottom and instinctively pulled back. My pointer finger got caught on her suit, and down they came. I was now face-to-face (maybe a foot or so away) from my cousin's vagina. This time, I was not as shocked as I had seen this not too long ago. She pulled up her bottoms and swam away, like nothing happened. To this day, neither had ever spoken about this situation. I guess the cat is out of the bag now.

Fast-forward a year or so. Three to four of us were sitting on a park bench across the street from my house. We were waiting for the weather to clear a bit so we could get in our daily baseball game. Sitting on the bench with us was an eighth-grade girl named Kathy. She was a year older than us and quite flirtatious. It was raining ever so slightly. She was wearing cutoff jean shorts and a white blouse. As her blouse got wet from the rain, we could all see through to her frilly white bra. She had the biggest set of breasts in the entire eighth-grade class. One of my buddies picked up a worm and threw it down her top. She giggled and squealed. "Get it out! Get it out!" she screamed. He proceeded to put his hand down her top, searching everywhere for that worm. After a few minutes, he retrieved the worm, smiling from ear to ear. He then handed it off to the next guy who proceeded to do the same thing. Finally, it was my turn. In it went. I put my hand down her top to begin my search. I was embarrassed and excited all at the same time. I was grabbing anything and everything. I eventually found the worm and removed my hand from Kathy's top. My first encounter with a real breast! I've got to tell you, it still remains one of the most erotic events in my little pea brain.

Not every early sexual experience was positive. The last story I would like to share with you from this earlier period of my life involved my mother and me. Hold tight, you sick bastards, it's not what you think. Fast-forward an additional year (eighth grade). My body and mind were definitely going through changes. We learned a bit about puberty at school, just enough to confuse the hell out of us. I was starting to grow hair in places I never had before. My voice was starting to crack and get deeper. My penis was starting to expand and contract at a moment's notice, just like the guy I saw several years ago. I was starting to pay much closer attention to the opposite sex. I didn't understand the thoughts/feeling, but I loved them! One day, after a long day of baseball, football, whatever, I showered up and headed off to bed. As I crawled under the covers, I heard a loud crunching noise. As I rolled back and forth, the noise continued.

What the hell was that? I pulled off the corner of my sheet to expose a second sheet made of plastic. It was covering the entire mattress. What the hell was this for? I was too tired to care much about it that evening. The next morning, I approached my mom. I asked her what the plastic sheet was for.

"To keep your bed clean at all times."

I reminded her I take a shower every night and that I was always clean as a whistle when I went to bed. She just smiled back at me, not saying another word. I asked several more times without a response. I was confused. Every night thereafter, I encountered that sheet. It was driving me crazy. After several weeks, I told my buddies. Most were just as confused. One, however, was not. Apparently, his mother did the same thing with his bed. He went on to say, "It's to protect your bed from wet dreams."

"Wet dreams? Are kids drinking in bed while they're half asleep? Are we drooling so much at night that we are damaging our mattresses?"

He then proceeded to tell us about how we have erotic dreams that result in us ejaculating in our pants and onto the sheets. Erotic dreams? Ejaculation? All new words to me. I had a hard time processing this information. Over the next several years, I would eventually fill in all the gaps, no thanks to my parents. Speaking about sex in my house was taboo. Unlike in the movies, there was *never* the birds and the bees moment with either my father or mother. What I learned about sex was picked up from my friends (generally their older brothers) or through my own experimentation later on in life. The story of my life.

*****

At this point in my tale, I feel it's pertinent to share a story with you. Although I'm gaining more confidence as the months and years go by, there are moments of serious digression. This is a big one. It was now February of 1974. I was lazily looking out the window of my sixth-grade classroom, watching the snow fall. It was a typical winter's day on the Northwest Side of Chicago. To say I was bored and disengaged was the understatement of the year. Mr. Fisher, our homeroom teacher, was reading all the day's announcements.

"Blah, blah, blah..."

What's this I hear? Camp who? When? My focus had immediately returned back to Mr. Fisher.

"Representatives from Camp Odessy will be on site this afternoon to talk about their summer camp."

Summer camp? As he spoke, he pointed to an oversized poster in the back of the classroom that I inadvertently missed in my earlier, zombielike state. Prior to the start of our next class, I made an immediate beeline to the back of the class to check this out further. The poster contained the most beautiful pictures of sunsets, campfires, shooting stars, etc. that I had ever seen. There were smiling faces everywhere. I was hooked. As I proceeded through each of my remaining classes, I could not stop thinking about what I saw and heard earlier. We finally reached the end of our school day and were marched into the lunchroom for the formal camp presentation. In walked two of the most beautiful people I had ever seen in my life—a man and a woman, eighteen to twenty-one years of age, both dressed in their blue-and-white-striped Camp Odessy shirts, bright white tennis shoes and teeth, hair perfect. Ken and Barbie had descended on St. Ladislaus grade school to make their sales pitch! They went up and down the aisles, handing out professionally done brochures, talking about what a wonderful opportunity it would be for city slickers like ourselves to enjoy a week at summer camp. It turned out they were both counselors and were speaking from firsthand experience. Sailing, fishing, hiking, archery, etc., all under the guidance of Ken and Barbie. How do you beat that? I was hooked. I couldn't wait to go home and talk to my parents about this once-in-a-lifetime opportunity. Of course, I must first speak to my best bud, Ricky, to make sure he was on board. How amazing would it be to be part of this together? Of course, he was game. We set our strategies and headed home to begin negotiations. After much back-and-forth with our parents (which included begging, crying, silent treatment, etc.), they reluctantly agreed to let us go. My heart and head were soaring. June (the first week to be precise) would not get here soon enough.

Fast-forward to Saturday morning, June 1, 1974. Ricky and myself had been loaded into the back of my parents' car to make the trip down to the South Side of Chicago (Evergreen Park), where we would be catching the bus to take us to camp. Camp was a five- to six-hour ride, due south, into the beautiful Ozark region of the state. No big deal. I saw the pictures of the state-of-the-art, fully air-conditioned buses we would be traveling in. As we pulled into the lot, we saw kids and parents everywhere. It was total chaos. My parents, wanting to beat any kind of traffic home, dropped us off in the middle of this mess to fend for ourselves. We began our search for someone, anyone, in charge. We finally located a person in faded Odessy garb who appeared to be in charge. His name was Joe, and he was one of our camp counselors. What the hell happened to Ken and Barbie? This guy looked like some kind of hobo who just jumped off a passing freight train. He brought us over to a group of forty to fifty kids standing in the corner of the parking lot.

"Stay here and wait for your bus to arrive," he said. We reluctantly agreed as we both looked over our shoulders to watch my parents' car zoom out of site.

"Calm down," I told myself. "You're just nervous because this is the first time you have been away from your parents. It's all good. No need to worry." I was feeling much better about the situation until I saw a line of yellow-and-black school buses making their way across the parking lot. That couldn't be for us? These must be for another group. Guess again. On the side of the bus, where the company name was generally located, was a rectangular piece of cardboard that said Camp Odessy. Son of a bitch. No Ken and Barbie—strike 1. No air-conditioned buses—strike 2. This was not starting off well. A few more hippies, in blue-and-white shirts, appeared from nowhere and started loading us onto the buses. The first of many tears to come started welling up in my right eye. Thank God Ricky was there.

The buses were loaded, and the caravan started heading south. It was early. We'd had no breakfast. For some unknown reason, the windows in the bus were all closed. It did not take long before the first kid was puking in the front row. I burrowed further down into my seat. I hummed to myself, trying to block out the sound. A second kid started up. Then a third. It was like a tidal wave that could not be stopped. The sights, the sounds, the smell consumed me. I had lost all control. I began to projectile vomit last night's dinner all over the seat in front of me. It ricocheted off the seat cushion and blasted off my face, resulting in several more rounds. No one came to help. No one was there to clean us up. We were on our own. As you will see, this will be an all too familiar position for the balance of the week.

Upon completion (seemed like hours), I decided to take my shirt off, cleaned myself the best I could and stuffed it under the seat. Now I got the privilege of smelling that for the balance of the trip. Here's where it gets interesting. We were about halfway to our destination when one of the brainiac hippies decided it was time to serve lunch on the bus. Spam sandwiches and warm pink lemonade for all! I'd never heard of Spam. I'd never eaten Spam. I had no idea what the hell it was until I peeled back the wrapping. Oh my god, it looked like brain matter. Again, someone started retching up front, and before you know it, round 2 was in full swing, including myself. With no shirt to clean up with, I took off my socks and did what I could (pretty resourceful, aren't I?).

At approximately 1:00 p.m. on Saturday, our bus pulled into the lot of our final destination. We had arrived at Camp Odessy. At first glance, it looked like a very rundown concentration camp—a big gravel lot, several gray and black outbuildings, a flagpole with no flag. It was cold. It was foggy. I immediately said to myself, "I love my parents, and I want to go home." But there was no going home. *You spent weeks working over your parents so you can attend this camp. You're six hours away from home, certainly too far for your parent to drive and pick you up. No, sir, you're in for the long haul.*

The hippie camp counselors began taking us off the buses and dividing us into groups. We were looking at approximately twenty groups, twenty-five to thirty kids in each group. Ricky and I had several "normal" housing options to choose from (cabins, tents, etc.). Being the adventurers that we were, we opted for the tree house option. It looked outstanding in the brochure. Our counselor, Billy (good hobo/redneck name), gathered up his fledglings and started down the trail to our new home. Mind you, I use the term *trail* loosely. It was more of a beaten path. Approximately forty-five minutes from camp central, we arrived at our tree house estate. Up in the trees, anywhere from one to two stories off the ground, were four plywood "boxes." I used the word *box* because I struggled with finding any other word to describe them. There was a wooden ladder, hammered into the tree, that lead up to each. There was a wooden walkway connecting each of the boxes to one another. The front of each of the boxes were open, leaving all of us exposed to the elements. In each of the boxes were triple bunk beds on both sides, allowing for six campers to a box.

"Welcome to your new home, boys," Billy said.

Another tear began to well up in my right eye. We all picked a box and headed up to get situated. Ricky and I chose box 2, bunks 5 and 6 (top two bunks), thinking the higher off the ground we were, the farther away we would be from any pests. *Please. You're in the middle of the woods in an open plywood box. Do you really think you'd be safe anywhere?* We climbed up to our bunks, which were nothing more than horizontal planks of plywood. We stored our duffel bags, laid out our sleeping bags, and crawled back down to begin our adventure. Billy provided us with a very crude map of the grounds and headed off down the path.

"See you at dinner, boys."

Although it was somewhat cold and still a bit foggy, Ricky and I decided we'd get into our bathing suits, do some exploring, and try to get a swim in at Lake Odessy. Off we went, map in hand, excited about the adventures that lay ahead. We reached Lake Odessy in about thirty minutes. On the shore were two sailboats, a bit different-looking than the ones in the brochure. The paint was faded on both. One was missing a mast completely. The other was entirely filled with water, with a hole the size of my fist on its side. So much for sailing. We decided as long as we had our suits on, and we were here at the lake, the least we could do was go for a dip. We dove in. Again, not the bright-blue waters in the brochure but refreshing just the same, especially since you were still covered in your own puke from the bus ride down. I was out about fifty yards from shore when I spotted some movement in the water. I had no idea what it was, but it was coming straight at me. As it came into focus, it appeared to be a snake. City boy. Snake. I screamed like a little schoolgirl and hauled my ass to the shore. A few of our fellow camp members were on shore, laughing their asses off, asking me if I'd ever seen a water moccasin before. What the hell was a water moccasin? Another tear appeared in my right eye. Seeing we weren't bright enough to bring something to dry off with, we began pushing water off our skin with our hands. I was noticing I had black bumps on my legs, torso, and arms. The same jokers that told us about the water moccasins were now giving us a lesson in what leaches were. City boy. Leaches. Holy shit. Where the hell am I? We spent the next thirty minutes peeling each of the bloodsuckers from our skin.

Ricky and I, along with the rest of the campers, spent the rest of the day wandering aimlessly. No supervision. No agenda. No planned activities. We all eventually made our way back to base camp. A bell rang, and we were told it was suppertime. We followed the masses into one of the outbuildings. There were rows of picnic tables. On each table was a jug of pink lemonade, the same lemonade we had on the bus. I was feeling sick just looking at it. As we sat down, fellow campers were coming out of the kitchen with platters full of what appeared to be hamburgers. Thank God because I was starving. One bite into the sandwich told me this was unlike any hamburger I'd had in the past. I peeled back the bun to discover I was eating charbroiled Spam. Not again. I spat it back out just in time to wipe the next tear from my eye.

Billy's boss made an announcement to the entire group of campers. "Part of your team's responsibilities this week will be for the preparation, distribution, and cleanup of all meals."

What? Not only do I have to eat this shit, I actually have to prepare and serve it? Another tear appeared.

As dinner was cleared away by the first group of fellow campers, another announcement was made. Tomorrow night, we would be partaking in a game called Cowboys and Indians. What now? We headed back to our tree houses. Cold. Sick. Hungry. With no mother (or camp counselor for that matter) to provide us with any type of guidance, we decided the smart thing to do was live in our wet bathing suits all week. We climbed into our bunks to try to get some sleep. All I could here was the low-level whimpers of my fellow campers as we all tried to get some sleep. I guess I was not alone. We woke bright and early to discover several campers went MIA during the night. Apparently, they wandered back to camp and called their parents to come get them. All I could think was, *You lucky SOBs.*

Day 2 was like day 1. No organized activities. No supervision. Just a bunch of grade school boys wandering the Ozarks. We passed the time by playing a game called chicken with our pocket knives. Yes, we all had knives. It was one of the items we were told to bring with our camping gear. I was not sure why. We never did anything with them except to play chicken. The rules of chicken were simple. Throw the knife as close as you can to the other person's foot without hitting them. You would be declared the chicken if you moved your foot. Needless to say, we had a few "minor" injuries throughout the week.

Fast-forward to 9:00 p.m. that evening. Time for the Cowboy and Indian game. There would be one group called the Cowboys. Their job would be to move a mattress from point A to point B without being caught by any of the Indians. All the rest of us were Indians. All the Indians were provided a feather that they were to wear on their heads, signifying they were an Indian. As a fellow Indian, you can steal the feather from any other Indian, removing them from the game. We were scattered throughout the woods. Nobody was provided a flashlight. It was pitch-black. It was freezing, especially because we were still running around in our wet suits. A horn sounded in the distance to mark the beginning of the game. Within seconds, Ricky and I heard some kids hauling ass and screaming at the top of their lungs. We started running like hell. I hit a tree stump and went down immediately. As I was fumbling in the darkness, the screaming got louder and closer. *Rip.* My feather was gone, along with a portion of my scalp. My leg was torn to shit. My head was bleeding from where my feather was. It was dark, and I wanted to go home. I picked myself up and started walking in what I believe was the direction of the camp. In approximately a hundred yards or so, I ran into Ricky, basically in the same condition as I was. *Don't worry, Ricky, I can read your mind.* We walked for what seemed like hours. Suddenly, off in the distance, we heard the sound of a siren. It got closer, stopped, picked up again, and then faded away. Shortly thereafter, the sound of the dinner bell could be heard. We followed that sound into camp. It turned out the siren that we heard was from an ambulance, taking one of our fellow campers off to the hospital with a broken leg. Seemed he was hauling ass from some other screaming Indians when he fell off a ledge in the darkness. *What kind of crazy camp is this? Where the hell am I? I want my mommy.*

Let's fast-forward to Wednesday afternoon. We were five days into our adventures now, and it was more of the same. We were still living in our wet suits. Nobody had changed clothes all week, so we were beyond chafing at this point. Safe to say, all our assholes were bleeding. Nothing but Spam and lemonade all week. By the way, did I mention we discovered another critter that would scare the shit out of any city boy? Ticks—insects that burrow into your skin until you go insane. How did I find out about ticks? One of our fellow campers decided to show us a tick on his dick. Twenty or so twelve-year-old campers stood around looking at a fellow camper's tool with a tick in it. You can't make this shit up.

Back to my original point of this story. Tree houses don't have bathrooms. Being from the city, I'd never shit in the woods, let alone an outhouse. I made up my mind, early on in this adventure, that I was not going to take a shit all week. I'd hold it until I get home. Let me tell you something. That was not possible after eating Spam five days in a row. My insides were churning. Something had to give. It was at that point I remembered there was a set of flush toilets at base camp. I'd walk the mile or so in, relieve myself, and head on back. Perfect plan. The problem began upon my arrival at the washroom. It turned out I was not the only camper with this same idea. All three stalls were busy with at least six to eight guys sitting on a bench in front of the stalls. I took my seat on the bench. My stomach was rumbling. Everyone was talking about how they needed to take a healthy one. My mind went into overdrive. I could not hold it any longer. I headed out to the back side of the outhouse, dropped my wet bathing suit, and began taking a shit. It turned out that there was a twelve- to eighteen-inch crack between the wall of the bathroom and the floor where light could show through.

Somebody yelled, "Look, somebody's taking a shit outside!"

I fucking panicked. I was halfway through taking a shit as I heard an army of guys tearing out of the washroom. What could I do? Turned out the bathroom was up on a hill. I immediately started barrel-rolling down the hill, maybe ten to fifteen turns before I came to a stop. I immediately covered myself up with leaves, sticks, or whatever was around me. I now lay motionless, looking up at the building. I was totally camouflaged as I looked up at the six to eight campers who were now standing and pointing at my shit. They were walking around the building, pointing off in the distance. They couldn't see me! I pulled it off. I continued to lay motionless until everybody cleared out. My joy soon turned to sorrow as I then realized I was covered in my own shit with no access to any soap or shower. I made my way across camp, jumped into the leach-filled lake, and cleaned myself off the best I could. Needless to say, I literally found shit behind my ears when I finally did take a shower at home.

It was finally Saturday morning. Somehow, we had survived our week at Camp Hell. The bus to Chicago would be leaving after breakfast. You guessed it, Spam and eggs. Billy, the counselor we had rarely seen all week, yelled out to me to start serving breakfast. Just my luck. I ended up having to do this crap on the last day. Such was life. I served and cleaned up as quickly as I could. I grabbed my bag (entirely full of clean clothes because I was still wearing my wet, shit-ridden clothes) and headed for the lot. There were yellow school buses everywhere with no one there to provide directions on where to go. I ran into a guy we met during the week, and he proceeded to say, "What are you still doing here? Your bus for Chicago left ten minutes ago."

Fuck, the tear in the right eye, crap. I was now full-out bawling like a schoolgirl. I missed my bus, and I was stuck at Camp Hell! Suddenly, I looked up, and I saw Ricky waving at me from a bus window. It was like I saw an angel. I climbed onto that bus, thanked God from the bottom of my heart, and prepared for the long ride home. Upon arrival, I scanned the parking lot for my parents. *There they are!* I bolted from the bus into my mom's awaiting arms. My face was flush. I was crying uncontrollably. I reeked of shit. So much for that tough-guy, macho shit behavior. I crawled into the back seat of my father's car and passed out for the long ride home. Thank God my nightmare was over!

*****

It was now the fall of 1975. I was heading into eighth grade, my final year at St. Ladislaus. Thanks to my exposure to heavy metal music, I'd gone from this skinny, wimpy little shit to this energetic, confident, outgoing young boy. It would be safe to say, without any arrogance, that I was one of the most popular kids in my eighth-grade class. Funny, athletic, good-looking—what could I possibly do to take me to the next level? Over the past two years, I served as a patrol guard. We were assigned a specific corner and were responsible for safely crossing our fellow students. We were all given an orange belt that we wore across our chests and waists so proudly. In seventh grade, I served as the assistant patrol captain, along with two of my fellow classmates. We got to roam the streets, making sure the crossing guards were doing their jobs correctly. A position of authority. When the patrol captains a year ahead of us graduated, we bought each of them a top-of-the-line radio as their parting gift. How cool was that! With the position now vacated, I applied and was given the patrol captain position. It was the pinnacle of my eighth-grade career. I'd make out the crossing guard assignments every week. I would check on each station, along with my two cocaptains. I was even allowed to leave church early (what a bonus!) to make sure everything was in order. It doesn't get any better than that.

Throughout the year, all I could think about was the cool gift I was going to receive at year-end. I dreamed about it. I obsessed over it. What would it be? Throughout the year, I did my job with passion and a sense of responsibility. I was going to be the best captain ever, which would result in the best gift ever! It was now May, and it was time for our thank-you party. What could it be? A radio? A new baseball mitt? As we were each handed our gifts, my heart immediately sank. I could tell by its feel it was a clothes box. Shit! We tore through the wrapping paper, opened the top, and found a pair of brown corduroy pants. Fuck! A year's worth of work and sacrifice for a pair of corduroy pants! I was beyond disappointed, beyond angry. I won't kid you. My cheeks were bright red, and I could feel my eyes swelling with tears. I pushed everything back as I choked out a "Thank you."

I left the building, my level of anger off the charts. At least I had an intramural hockey game to look forward to. Reminder, we played these games on an asphalt parking lot at school. Generally, I went home before the game to change into my hockey stuff (blue jeans, T-shirt, and gym shoes). Not today! Today I was changing into my corduroy pants and heading over in my white button-down school shirt and leather shoes. As I mentioned earlier, we played all sporting events with no fear, no holding back. We played to win at all costs. Today was no different. In fact, I was playing at a much higher level due to the amount of anger and energy built up earlier. I was diving. I was sliding. I was hacking. We proceeded to kick the living shit out of our opponent. Half the buttons on my shirt were torn off. I had huge holes in both the knees on my pants. I had broken off a heel on my right shoe. I headed home after the game, stripped my clothes and shoes off, and threw them in the garbage. I could not be happier! I could not think of a better send-off from my grade school. Let's enjoy the summer of 1976 and get ready for high school. Enough of this kid shit!

I'm A Problem Child

1976–1977

Grade school was in the rearview mirror. I was so excited to be going off to high school in the next few weeks. The only negative was, my parents decided to send me to St. Patrick, an all-boys school run by the Christian Brothers. If you think the nuns at St. Ladislaus were crazy/strict, you've got another thing coming. The other problem was, St. Patrick was not the "cool" school. That would be Holy Cross. The majority of my grade school friends went to Holy Cross. A few of the remaining fags made their way to St. Pat's. I was fortunate that one of my best friends at the time, Ted, was joining me. At least I knew someone.

The first day of school arrived. As expected, it was total chaos. Due to numerous conflicts in schedule, my parents were unable to take me to any of the orientation programs over the holiday. I was stepping foot in the building for the very first time. My grade school was much smaller in comparison. This was a three-story building with dozens upon dozens of classrooms, not to mention a gym, library, pool, etc. I didn't have my schedule. I didn't know where I was supposed to be. All of a sudden, I was not that tough eighth-grade boy anymore. Once again, my face was flushed, and I felt a tear forming in my right eye. I made my way to the front office. I told them of my tale. After some paper pushing and desk door slamming, the brother handed me a copy of my schedule, along with a map of the school and said, "Good luck!"

I headed off in search of my first class. I finally found the room and slid in. The brother teaching the class stopped to ask me what my name was and why I was late. I began to explain myself when he said, "Silence!" He called me up to the front of the class and told me to put my hands on his desk. I complied immediately because I was scared shitless. He pulled out a paddle, twenty-four inches long, eight inches wide, and two inches thick with holes drilled through it top to bottom. He took that paddle back and connected with my ass at full throttle. He almost knocked me across the top of the desk. Once again, I could feel tears welling up in my eyes, a combination of pain and embarrassment. I was told to take my seat, shut up, and never be late for this class again. I was not even through the first hour of my day, and I was already in trouble. Not good.

The bell rang, and it was time to move on to my second class of the day. You had approximately five minutes to get from point A to point B. Once again, I had no idea where I was going. I took my map and began walking fast to assure I was not late once again. All of a sudden, I heard a whistle, followed by a shout. "Stop!" *Are you talking to me?* It was what you call a hall monitor. He informed me that there was no running in the halls, and he proceeded to write me up for the infraction. By the time this wrapped up and I found my second class, I was late once again. This time, the brother read me the riot act and issued me a detention slip. I was to report to detention one hour early tomorrow morning. (Regular start time was 8:00 a.m.; I was to be in detention at 7:00 a.m. and, God forbid, not be late).

As if my day could not get any worse, third period was swim class. I headed to my locker, grabbed my swimsuit and towel, and made my way to the pool locker room *on time*! I was so proud of myself. There were forty to fifty boys in the locker room when the brother teaching the class arrived. He told us to get changed and report to the pool for laps immediately. We all changed into our suits and scooted out to the pool. We stood in a straight line, side by side, as the brother came out of his office. He smiled and shook his head. He began to speak, "Gentlemen, I don't think you understand. This is not your local swimming hole. This is St. Patrick's world-class swimming pool. We will never take a chance of clogging the filters by allowing any type of cloth contaminant to clog our filters. Everyone, back into the locker room to remove your suits and return to the pool. Now!"

We all froze. Did we hear him right? We were going to swim naked for the next fifty minutes. We all marched back into the locker room, not a word spoken. We dropped our drawers, wrapped a towel around our naked bodies, and headed back out. Once again, the brother stepped out from his office, and he was pissed.

"Towels on the bench, boys! Seeing you can't follow instructions properly, you are all going to give me three laps around the pool while duckwalking!"

What the hell was duckwalking? After a brief explanation, it became quite clear. You are to squat down, your butt two to three inches off the ground, and proceed to put one foot in front of the other. Just imagine forty freshman boys naked, duckwalking in circles around the pool, one right behind the next. It took us five to ten minutes to complete this exercise. Once completed, we were told to line up for roll call.

At this point in our lives, it did not take much for a young boy to get an erection. A dirty thought, a slight breeze against your penis, whatever. I immediately tried to put a bad thought in my dream. I repeated to myself, "Think of your grandma in her old-lady underwear." Over and over and over. *It's working. Thank God!* Some of the other boys were not as fortunate. As someone got an erection, the others screamed and pointed it out to the remaining classmates. They had now been targeted as a fag and would be dealt with appropriately. After we finished our laps, we had ten minutes of free time. Do you really expect us to jump around and play in the pool *naked*? We actually used that last ten minutes to kick the crap out of the pool fags, nearly drowning them to death in the process. Where was the supervision? Where was the brother now?

Before I leave this subject, there are a few more facts that I need to share with you. One, each boy is expected to buy a bright-green (color of the school) swim cap to be worn at all times while in the pool. We don't want our long hair to clog those precious filters. Add that to your mental picture. It gets worse. God forbid, you forget your swim cap. The brother will be more than happy to provide you with a cap to borrow for the day. Its base color is yellow with lots of pretty pink, blue, and white flowers. The punishment does not end there. Before class officially starts, you must duckwalk around the pool, with the ladies' swim cap on in front of all your classmates. *Slightly* embarrassing, don't you think? I wonder how many of my fellow classmates were scarred for life. I know I'll never forget it.

Finally, back to the erection situation. There was one boy who could not control himself on a daily basis. As a result, he was getting his ass kicked every day. One day, he retaliated in a big way. He went back to the locker room, shit on his hand, and started throwing his crap in all direction. We all ducked for cover. I was hit! Dear Lord, I've got someone else's shit in my hair and on my cheek! As my fellow classmates were pummeling this poor guy, I was at the sink washing shit out of my hair and off my face. Welcome, my friend, to your freshman year at St. Pat's.

*****

St. Pat's had so many rules that I could not keep track of them. All I know was, I was in trouble all the time. Serving detention went from once a week to several days of the week to every day of the school year. Going to school at 7:00 a.m. became the daily routine for me for the rest of my high school career. The biggest issue I had was with their policy regarding the acceptable length of your hair. Bottom line was, your hair could not touch the back of your collar. Are you kidding me? In the mid to latter part of the '70s, everyone wore their hair long. All my buddies. All the rock stars I idolized—Stevie, Ricky, and Gary—for God's sake. I refused to cut my hair. I would not do it. That was one of the main reasons for me spending all that time in detention. It was a principle, not principal. I had my own assigned seat. I was surrounded by my fellow troublemakers/rebels, and I loved it! We did whatever we liked and were glad to accept our punishment. The strangest thing was, the school never alerted my parents of this situation. No note was ever sent home. No discussion during any parent-teacher conferences. Nothing. It was my little secret. It was not until my senior year that my parents found out what had been going on. By then, who really gives a shit?

*****

My buddy Ted and I were inseparable at this point. We hung out at lunch. We hung out after school. We pretty much did everything together. The problem was, we were very bad influences on each other. Case in point. We walked home down Belmont Avenue East every day after school. We walked by store after store for several blocks until we made the north hand turn toward home. Every day, we would stop by Goldblatt's to buy a bag of chips and something to drink. The problem with that was, we didn't have a ton of money, so our funds got depleted very quickly. We decided to go for plan B. While one person waited outside, the other would head in, grab what we wanted to eat, and head back out as quickly as possible. We figured if we switched positions every other day, they'd never catch on. Ted went first. Within two minutes, we were back on the street eating Funyuns and drinking chocolate milk. Success! The second day was my turn. Through the front door, hang a left, head to the racks and coolers, grab the booty, and retrace your steps as quickly as possible. I was out! I was excited, even euphoric. At first, we hid the snacks under our shirts and coats. As time progressed, we got more ballsy. We walked right in, grabbed the stuff, and walked right out. We made no attempt to hide what we were doing. Our thought process was, if you acted like everything was normal, who the hell was going to question you? I hate to say it, but it worked. This went on for the balance of the school year. Almost a daily occurrence. We never got stopped. Ever!

We decided, based on our earlier successes, to up the ante. We were now shoplifting anything we wanted or needed. Clothes, records, shoes, etc. Nothing was off-limits. We were totally out of control but could not help ourselves. We were both born and raised

Catholic. We knew the Ten Commandments backward and forward. "Thou shall not steal." Do you think I give a shit? It became part of our everyday lives. We didn't think about the impact it might be having on the poor people who own these stores. We didn't worry about going to hell, as hell was the furthest thing from our mind. It was fun. It was exciting. It was free.

One day, I crossed a line. There was a small shop on Belmont Avenue called Metro. They sold a bit of everything, including sporting equipment. To this point in my life, I was still using the borrowed baseball mitt I obtained several years ago. It did the job, but I felt it was time for a new one. I put it on my "shopping" list. I headed over to Metro. I walked in, pretended to look at this and that, then headed over to the sporting goods section. I found the exact glove I was looking for. I scanned the area, nobody in sight. I grabbed the mitt and headed straight for the exit. I was in luck. There was a young girl manning the register. She was chewing gum, head down, reading some kind of book or magazine. I headed through the front door, hooked up with Ted, and started walking west at a brisk pace. I was smiling from ear to ear, laughing and joking as we went. All of a sudden, we heard a deep voice, "Stop! Thief!" We turned around and saw this huge guy hauling ass toward us. We took off in a sprint. He was big. He was fast. We raced down the block with him close on our tails.

What the hell are we going to do? I thought fast. My buddy Tony lived on the next block over. If we could get to his house, maybe he'd let us in. We were on his front porch in a millisecond. We proceeded to ring the bell over and over. No answer. The guy chasing us was coming through the gangway between houses. No time to waste. We burst through the front door and up the flight of stairs in front of us. (Note: Tony lived on the second floor of a typical Chicago two-flat.) The guy was just hitting the front door. We crashed into Tony's house. To the right, Tony's father was lying on the couch, asleep. We blasted through the hallway/kitchen and made our way to the back exit. We heard a scream coming from his mother. She must have caught a brief glimpse of our backsides heading through the back exit. We heard some crashing noises followed by Tony's father's going fucking nuts. Apparently, he woke up and caught this guy tearing through his house, his wife screaming in the background. All hell must have broken out. I didn't care. I was not sticking around to find out. We blasted through the back door and ran all the way home. We sat down and talked about our grand adventure. We dodged a bullet, and I had my new baseball mitt. It doesn't get any better than that!

*****

By this point in life, I had upgraded from my weekly *Leader* newspaper route to delivering the *Chicago Tribune* on a daily basis. More responsibility. Longer route. More money. I didn't mind the hard work as the money was good. Not as rewarding as stealing, but it put much-needed cash in my pocket. I'd been doing this for several years now without a problem. Enter Ted once again. He came up with an outstanding idea.

"You don't need to work this chicken shit job anymore. It's time to move onto bigger and better things."

Of course, we never got around to talking about those "better" things. All we talked about was how to quit this job and land a big score. We decided the best thing to do was to finish the month out, collect the money, get my final payout, and quit. But there was a catch. We waited for the new kid to deliver papers for the next three weeks, and during the week prior to the standard collection day, I hit all the customers and collect this poor kid's money. The people still knew me and trusted me. So what if I was a week early? They'd never know. They'd never question. I headed on out. The plan worked like a charm. I ended up pulling in almost $100. Let's not forget about the almost $40 in tips! Not too shabby. The *Tribune* never called. The kid never attempted to track me down. I cleared $140 and blazed on. I added another dozen Hail Marys to my never-ending penance.

*****

It got better, only this time, it was with my other best friend Ricky. At this point in our life, we just loved walking the streets and back alleys of Chicago. Every time we headed out, we pushed our boundaries further and further. There was nowhere we wouldn't go and check out. On one of our typical patrols, we came across a TV sales and repair shop. For some odd reason, we noticed there were several bricks missing from the back wall of the building. We investigated. As we got closer, we realized we could peer into the shop through the hole. As you scanned the area, you could make out the new, used, and under-repair television sets. Our eyes lit up. At this point, we hatched a plan to get into the store, steal a few sets, and head back home. Our adrenaline was rushing. We tore at the hole in the wall. Brick after brick was pried loose until an opening was created for our skinny asses to squeeze through. We were in! We stumbled around in the dark. With what little light was available, we looked at each of the sets. We each picked one out, and the two of us moved them to the opening. Ricky slid through the opening and prepared to receive the sets. It took me several minutes (due to the weight and size) to shimmy the first set up the wall and out the hole, into Ricky's waiting arms. I did the same with the second set. Once complete, I crawled back through the hole and met up with Ricky on the outside. We were both smiling from ear to ear. We had visions of watching each of these beautiful TVs in our bedrooms. The first kids at our age to have a TV in our rooms! (Unheard of at this time, but common practice now.)

Suddenly, the realization of the situation set in. *How are we going to get these huge TVs home?* It was going to take the two of us to carry each of these home. We were a good mile away from our destination. Someone was bound to see us and question what the hell we were doing. The other issue was, what we would tell our parents when we walk into our houses carrying brand-new TV sets (better than the sets either of our parents own at the present time). TVs just don't fall out of the sky. I guess we didn't think it all the way through. After much discussion back and forth, we decide we could not take the sets with us. We wrote the word *sorry* in the dust on top of the sets and headed home. We were sad about our loss, but elated about our latest escapade. I only wished I could be there when the store owner arrived to find a hole in his wall and two brand-new TVs sitting in his back parking lot. The thought put a smile on my face as I drifted off to sleep.

*****

After the whole *Chicago Tribune* fiasco, it was time to find another job to put some cash back in my pocket. As I said earlier, I've learned that having your own money, at any age, provides you with both freedom and happiness (can't buy you happiness as a teenager, my ass!). I applied for and got my next job at Dunkin' Donuts. I was underage, so I lied on my application. Nobody bothered to check/verify. I was given the position of porter. Sounds important, doesn't it? Well, it's not. Turned out *porter* is another word for *slave labor*. I was the lowest link on the Dunkin' Donuts food chain. My job was to do the dishes, clean out the fryers, sweep and mop the floors, clean the restrooms, etc.—all the jobs nobody wanted to do. I didn't care. It was money in my pocket. The waitresses were cute. I had access to any type of doughnut-making materials, of which I took full advantage of. There was nothing better than a two-pound, one-foot-diameter Bismarck! I bit into that baby, and my head was full of cream. As the months went by, there was no limit to my imagination regarding the creations I came up with. This, somehow, helped to overshadow the horrific condition under which I was preforming my daily duties. There was not a day that went by that I was not soaked to the bone, stinking of fried dough. This went on for several months. I was getting bored. At this time, DD was running a promotion. Buy a coffee and/or doughnut and get a scratch card to win prizes—free food, cash, trips, etc. I'm sure you know where this is going. Being the little thief that I was, I started stealing some of these cards. A few here, a few there. I won a few bucks and some free doughnuts (which, for obvious reasons, I didn't need). I got greedy. One day, I stole a whole master carton of these tickets. Basically, the entire allotment for the store. The girls complained to the store manager. The storm manager investigated for about five minutes and determined I was the responsible party (duh). I was fired on the spot. I was sent home without pay. My porter days were over. As had been the pattern over my short life, there were no real repercussions for my unacceptable behavior or actions. This just emboldened me even further.

*****

Onto my next job. I secured a position at a place called Jan's Deli. It was a sandwich shop at the Harlem and Irving mall. I'd been hired as the salad maker. I'd never dealt with food products (doughnuts don't count as real food), let alone ever, *ever* prepared a salad. After a five-minute training session, I was off and running. The first few salads were an absolute train wreck. However, as time went by, my skills improved immensely. After several months, I thought I was BMOC (big man on campus). I wore my Jan's Deli uniform with pride (blue-and-white-striped vest, puffy chef's hat). Friends stopped in on a regular basis, and we shot the shit. I slid them free food through the side door. I myself pigged out on whatever I had access to—deli meats, cheeses, shrimp, desserts, etc. It was amazing I was not five hundred pounds. (I must have had a tapeworm back then!)

Fast-forward several months. I was able to get one of my high school buddies a job at the deli—assistant salad maker. My first direct report! I taught him the ropes, and we had a gas fucking around all afternoon. We entertained ourselves by throwing whole slabs of beef around like footballs. If it hit the floor, it was no big deal. Wipe it off and keep playing. Our favorite pastime was throwing butcher knives into full boxes and crates on the back wall. We drew bull's-eyes on each and did our best to hit it from different ranges. Who cared if we were tearing the shit out of whatever was in them? Of course, when asked what the hell happened, we raised our shoulders while working diligently on our salads. One day, my bud offered up a dare.

"Ten bucks says you can't smuggle out a bottle of booze from the front bar."

Yes, Jan's Deli had full stocked bar, and we had access to it. I took that bet and made my move. I went out behind the bar to change the garbage can bag out. While exiting, I grabbed a fifth of bourbon and dropped it into the bag. I walked through the swinging door and headed straight to the back exit to dump the garbage. I did it! I was in the money! I removed the bottle from the bag, hid it behind the dumpster (to retrieve later), dumped the trash, and headed back in. As I headed through the back door, I ran into my friend. He looked like he'd seen a ghost. I asked him what was wrong. Silence. Just then, the manager came busting through the door, a clipboard in one hand and a bottle of booze in the other.

"That looks a great deal like my bottle of booze."

"That's because it is, dumbass."

The manager escorted me into his office. He asked me several times if I stole that bottle.

I lied, "No, sir."

He finally lost his temper and said that I was fired. "Leave the store immediately, or I will call the police. You are banned from this deli, as well as the rest of the mall, indefinitely!"

I didn't mess around. I made an immediate beeline for the mall exit. As I hopped on the bus to head home, a familiar smile appeared on my face. Once again, I had gotten out of a bad situation without any negative repercussions. No police. No parents.

*****

As my freshman year at St. Pat's came to an end, my love of heavy metal music gained further momentum. It continued to fuel my fire, making me feel invincible. The harder, the heavier, and the faster the music was, the more I loved it, related to it. In addition to my ongoing exposure at Stevies House, I spent a *ton* of my free time at my absolute favorite record store—Rolling Stones. The outside of the store was covered with pictures and full-size cutouts of my favorite bands/band members. Walk inside, and the wall of heavy metal music hits you in the face like a sledgehammer. You are now looking at over five thousand square feet of albums from all around the world. If/when you find an album you like, you can bring it to the counter, and they play it over the speakers for you. Listen before you buy. I literally spent hours picking through the rows of albums, listening to tunes and making my final selection. This place was the closest thing to heaven that I had found to date. I could stay here forever, for God's sake! I headed home with my choices, looking forward to playing each on my shitty little turntable until my parents go nuts.

Nazareth.

Rainbow.

AC/DC.

Motorhead.

Van Halen.

King Diamond.

Saxon.

Raven.

The Runaways (who doesn't love an all-girls rock band?).

*****

The summer of 1977 was an absolute blast. My first year of high school was in the rearview mirror, and we had the next three months off, free to do whatever we wanted. No worries. Not a care in the world. My friends and I played sports eight to ten hours a day. The rest of the time we spent hanging out at the record shop or sitting on our front porches, shooting the shit. It was, without a doubt, the most carefree and relaxing times of our lives. There are two very memorable events from that summer that I would like to share with you. One June afternoon, my buddy Ted and I decided to take in a Cubs game. We jumped on the eastbound Addison bus at Central and headed down to Wrigley Field. We always got there hours early to watch batting practice and get as many autographs as possible. It was a beautiful day. The sun was shining. Not a cloud in the sky. As we headed up the steps, the field came into view. For anyone who's ever been to Wrigley Field in the daytime, they know what I'm seeing and experiencing. It's so beautiful! There are no words to describe it. It brings a tear to my eye just thinking about it now. It has the same effect on me now as it did so many years ago.

We immediately headed down to the left field wall. This was where a lot of the foul ball action happens. It was also a great place to talk to the players and try to secure autographs. We stood there for hours, diving after balls and securing several autographs. Suddenly, one of our favorite Cubs players at the time was walking by. José Cardenal! The place went crazy. Everybody was screaming at him, trying to get his attention. He looked over and smiled but made no movement toward the crowd. Ted and I continued to pester him.

"Please, José, please sign our program."

He waved us off. We kept pushing. He finally turned to us and, in broken English, said, "If you want an autograph, you'll need to come out here and get it from me." He was probably thinking that no way in God's greater earth were these kids going to come out there. Guess again. We immediately scaled the wall, dropped onto the field, and made our way to José. He couldn't believe it. His eyes were as wide as saucers. He proceeded to sign our cards, handed a baseball to Ted, and moved away quickly as the security guards rushed to constrain us. Six to eight big guys grabbed us and escorted us off the field in like ten seconds. A minute later, we were sitting in the Cubs' security office. Several high-level officials (we could tell because they were wearing vests with badges) were peppering us with questions.

"What're your names? How old are you? Why did you go onto the field?"

This went on for at least thirty minutes. As quickly as it started, the questioning stopped. They let us off with a warning and escorted us to the front gate. We wouldn't be seeing the game that day. We didn't care. We got José Cardenal's autograph, and that was all that mattered. Once again, no police got involved, and our parents were none the wiser.

*****

The second event involved my buddy Ricky. As you will see while reading the balance of this book, when he and I put our heads together, we generally come up with some very creative shit. This summer evening would be one such event. As we were walking in the neighborhood, we came across Winchell's Donuts. Yes, we once again found ourselves talking about doughnuts. Ricky asked me what we did at Dunkin' Donuts with the old doughnuts.

"Simple. We dumped them in the garbage cans out back."

We began talking about what a waste that was. It was such a shame that they couldn't be used for some other purpose. As strange as it sounded, we started feeling "sorry" for the poor, discarded doughnuts.

"What can we do to save them?"

"I got it. Let's rescue them from the dumpster!"

We proceeded to the back and pulled out two industrial-sized bags of doughnuts—old, greasy, full of frosting, jelly, custard, etc. Totally disgusting. We dragged the bags around with us all evening, trying to come up with a proper reuse. Got it! Why not throw these doughnuts at various targets throughout the neighborhood? We started with Winchell's. We set up shop across the street and started throwing doughnut after doughnut at the building, parking lot, parked cars, etc. *Splat! Smash! Pop!* It was raining doughnuts as we laughed our asses off. As people started to congregate in the parking lot to assess what was happening, we ran down the street laughing and screaming. We set up and went after our next most obvious targets—the beautiful public buses of the Chicago Transit Authority. We wiped out five to six buses over the next sixty minutes. We took the remaining doughnuts and hit anything in sight—mailboxes, garage doors, picture windows on storefronts, whatever. Such great fun! As we took our place on Ricky's front porch, we decided to come up with a name for this activity. After much back-and-forth, we settled on the Society for the Prevention of Cruelty to Doughnuts, or the SFTPOCTD. Perfect.

Several days later, we decided to take our show on the road. We turned to our buddy Tony, as he was the only one of driving age at this point. We headed over to the doughnut shop and grabbed the goodies. We threw a few here and there out the window, but it didn't provide the same excitement as the first time. We needed to up the ante. We headed over to the local Wendy's and placed our order. As we pulled up to pay and the pickup window opened, Ricky and I popped out the side windows of the car and started throwing doughnuts at the poor guy coming to take our money. We scored about four to five hits (face, head, chest, etc.) as Tony screamed out of the drive-through. We were in the back seat, laughing our asses off, screaming, "SFTPOCTD forever!" We didn't think twice about the poor kid we just attacked/humiliated. We were too caught up in our own little world to give a shit about anyone but ourselves. No one got Tony's license plate. No cops ever showed up at his front door. Once again, we got away with a bad deed with no repercussions. We were untouchable.

*****

That same summer, I decided to take a job working for my father. I would be a down and dirty laborer, working on one of his demolition crews. I didn't know a thing about demolition. What I did know was, my dad was willing to pay me $10 an hour cash, and I could work as many hours as I liked. I liked the sound of that. Just so I didn't have to do it solo, I talked my buddy Tony into working with me. We jumped on the Belmont bus and headed east toward the work site. With no guidance from my father on what to wear, we both had on cutoff shorts, T-shirts, and gym shoes. All the locations we would be working at were directly west of what they called Chicago's Gold Coast—all high-end homes in off-the-chart neighborhoods. My father was doing major-renovation work on each. He had a crew leader named Rick who oversaw the projects on a daily basis. We asked for him upon our arrival. Of course, the first thing he did was look us up and down and said, "What the fuck are you guys dressed up for, a day on the beach?" Of course, we had no idea what he was talking about. We had these puzzled looks on our faces. He said, "Okay, boys, well, it's your funeral." He handed us a hard hat, safety glasses, and a sledgehammer and escorted us into the home. His instructions were simple: "Tear the whole damn thing down! I want this building tore down to the studs and base floor. You are to move all material into that dumpster out back. Can you two idiots do that without killing each other?"

I looked at Tony, and he looked at me. We get $10 an hour to tear down houses? My god, what a beautiful thing! We picked up our sledgehammers and just went wild. We were talking and laughing the whole time we worked. For a hyperactive teenage boy full of energy and enthusiasm, you could not ask for a better situation.

We smashed. We pounded. We destroyed. Early on in the process, we figured out why shorts and T-shirts wouldn't cut it for this line of work. As we removed material to the dumpster, we inadvertently got cuts and bruises all over our bare skin. When the day was done, we both had wet and dried blood all over our bodies. We were full of dirt, grime, and dust from head to toe. We were sweating profusely, stinking to high heaven. As we walked to the bus stop, we were achy and tired but still damn excited about the new jobs we had. The bus arrived. We jumped on for the ride home. It was very crowded with people heading home for the night. As we made our way to the back of the bus, people were parting like the red sea. In fact, as luck would have it, two people on the right side of the bus vacated their seats immediately upon our arrival. Outstanding! We sat down, laid our heads back, and talked some more. That was interesting! As the bus moved away, more people around us were moving from their seats to assume a standing position at the front of the bus. What the hell was going on? As I looked over at Tony, the light bulb went off. These people weren't moving out of kindness. They were moving because we were absolutely filthy and stank like shit! At first, I was mortified. However, the longer I thought about it, the cooler I thought it was. I didn't give a shit about how I looked or smelled as long as I got a seat. Selfish SOB.

The following weeks, we changed to blue jeans, sweat shirts, and sturdier shoes. The one thing we didn't change was hopping on that bus daily, looking like the king and prince of the homeless squad. As we neared the end of summer, we were given our last assignment—full demolition of the second story on a house refurbishment. A wooden shoot was built from a second-story window into a dumpster below. All material was to be removed via that shoot. On occasion, that shoot got clogged, and we needed to crawl into the dumpster to clear it out. No big deal. One day, the shoot jammed, but we could not clear it. The material was halfway up and caught. We got a bright idea. Tony would climb into the shoot at the entrance, and I would hold him by his feet. And then he would hand the excess material back up to me. Sounds like a god plan. The problem was, Tony was a pretty big guy. As soon as he slid down, I was having one hell of a time holding onto him. I told him I couldn't do it. Unfortunately, I also didn't have the strength to pull him back up.

He was screaming, "Don't let go! I'll kill you if you let go!"

My arms began to shake. My hamstrings tightened. I couldn't hold on any longer. Tony slipped from my grip. *Crash!* He broke through the clog and got buried deep into the dumpster. After four to five minutes of thrashing around, he finally broke free. His face was red, covered with building materials from head to toe, his eyes wild like a rabid dog. Of course, I was in the window laughing my ass off.

"I'm going to kill you!" He came blasting out of the dumpster, making his way toward the second-floor entrance. There was a catch. We'd already demolished the entire first floor of the building, including the stairway. The only way up was via ladder. I ran to the opening and pulled the ladder up. Tony was swinging wildly at the end of the ladder, every four-letter wording streaming out of his mouth. I teased him. I lowered the ladder within inches of his reach just to pull it up again. He went crazy. I continued to laugh my ass off. This went on for fifteen to twenty minutes until we both tired of the exercise. I lowered the ladder down, and Tony climbed up. We sat in the corner of the room. A smile came to our faces as we broke into uncontrollable laughter. What a day!

*****

We all returned to school in the fall of 1977. Two of my best buddies, Ricky and Tony, headed off to Holy Cross, the cool all-boys high school. Ted, my other bud, and I headed off to St. Pat's to begin our sophomore year. Man, life was still good. I had a bank account full of cash I made over the summer. I was playing sports (organized, intramural, and pickup) of all kinds. I was in great shape. Not a care in the world. The only thing missing was a job. As I've said all along, money, at this point in my life, gave me the freedom to come and go as I pleased, buying whatever strikes my fancy.

I applied for a part-time stock boy position at Johnson Drugs. After a brief meeting/discussion with the assistant manager, I was offered the job and started immediately. It would be two part-time days during the week (after school) and weekends as necessary. It was perfect for me because I could still participate in the majority of my after-school activities (sports) while collecting a paycheck. I settled into a great routine—detention, school, sports, work, weekends with my friends. You couldn't beat that. As the months went by, I fell in love with my job. I did a bit of everything—unload trucks, stock the shelves, sweep and mop the floors. In addition, the people were absolutely outstanding. It was a mix of older women and kids my age. Some of the women acted as a mother figures toward me (not in a bad way but in a very caring, nurturing way, looking out for my best interests). The balance of the women treated me like their equals, like I was an adult. Some even flirted with me on occasion (very harmless), giving me a bigger head than I already had. The balance were teenagers, all of us within twenty-four months of one another. What a great mix. What a perfect "family." I could not begin to tell you how happy I was at this point in my life. I never wanted it to change. I was free. I was independent. I was "rich." My family life might be a bit fucked up, but I still had my surrogate family (school and neighborhood friends, coworkers, etc.). Little did I know what lay on the horizon. We'll get to that later on in the book.

*****

1977–1978

Winter of 1978, I have a few stories to share with you to help further define just how out of control we were at this point in our lives (remember, we are untouchable). The first started on a sunny day in late February. It was one of those rare days that Ricky, Tony, and I had a free afternoon after school. Tony was of driving age and swung by to pick us up. We cruised around a bit, discussing what we should do with the balance of our day. As we drove, we found ourselves driving east on Belmont Avenue. It just so happened that the entryway to St. Pat's was on the north side of the street a few blocks up. I told Tony to swing by to see if any of my friends were around. This is the point in the story where I need to fill you in on a key point. We (I'm not sure who the original owner was) owned a pellet gun. For whatever reason, that gun was stored in Tony's car (probably because we don't want our parents to find it) at all times. As we pulled up in front of my high school, I got the bright idea to pick up that gun, stick it out the window, and point it at a group of students waiting at the bus stop. Mind you, back then, you could not tell the difference between a pellet gun and a real gun. There were no bright markings to help distinguish one from the other. It was like a scene from a movie. Someone shouted out, "He has a gun!" In a split second, everyone was diving for cover, hands over their heads, screaming for their lives. We remained there for a few seconds then pulled away. I was laughing my ass off. Tony's eyes were like pin-wheels. He was having a hard time processing what just happened.

Ricky was in the back seat, quiet, just shaking his head. He knew I just fucked up big-time.

As we continue to drive east, a car sped up behind us. He was tailgating Tony, swerving back and forth. At first, we thought it was a pissed-off classmate of mine. Tony hit the gas and took off. We were turning left, then right on side streets, trying to shake this clown. It was not until the guy in the pursuing car slapped a blue strobe light (gumball) onto the roof of his car that we realized it was a cop. Holy shit! We were now screaming at one another, not knowing what to do. Tony continued to drive while I unloaded the pellets from the gun and chucked them out the window. We finally decided it was best to pull over and deal with this situation. Tony stopped the car. The guy in the pursuing car jumped out, pulled his weapon, and told me to step out of the car. I did not hesitate. As soon as I hit the pavement, he had me by the scruff of my neck and laid me out on the hood, spread-eagled. He was banging my head up and down as he frisked me. He put the cuffs on me and pushed me into the back of his unmarked squad car. Other police units arrived. One by one, Ricky and Tony were removed from the car and escorted into their own squad car.

As I was sitting there, pondering my fate, I was looking around, taking in my surroundings. I noticed there were a ton of high school girls standing around in their white blouses and plaid skirts. Upon further review, I realized we were being arrested in front of Notre Dame School for girls! Talk about insult to injury. A tow truck arrived to remove Tony's car from the middle of the street. The cars we were handcuffed in began to pull away. We started heading south down Austin Avenue. I was confused. I was familiar enough with the neighborhood to know the police station for Jefferson Park (my neighborhood) was north on Foster Avenue, not south. I asked the officer where he was taking me.

"To jail, smart-ass!"

I informed him he was going the wrong direction. Silence. Another fifteen minutes or so went by until we pulled into a parking lot next to an all-brick building, a sign hanging from its side that said Police. It was located on Madison Avenue on the west side of the city. It was one of the worst (most dangerous) neighborhoods in all of Chicagoland. We were each escorted from the vehicles, booked, and placed in holding cells. For some reason, based on age (I was the youngest), Ricky and Tony went into one area and I was placed in another. No special handling for us spoiled little white boys. Into general population for you. There was not another white person to be seen! God knows what these other detainees were in for. All I know was, I was scared shitless. Hours went by before someone screamed my name.

"Sorensen!"

I bolted up from my seat and headed to the door. I was escorted to an interview room. As the door opened, I saw my parents sitting at a desk across from the big burly cop who arrested me earlier. I took a seat next to my parents.

My father said, "Did you enjoy your time in jail, Bob? At the officer's advice, we let you sit there a few more hours to think about what you did."

Say what? I was a fifteen-year-old boy sitting in a jail cell with black murderers, rapists, child molesters, etc. Are you crazy? All this to teach me a lesson?

As the officer continued to talk, he pulled out a big manila envelope. He said, "Let me show you what your son had on his possession when we arrested him." He unsealed the envelop, and its contents spilled onto the desk—the pellet gun, a small box of pellets (damn, I forgot to toss those out the window), a buck knife (we all carried them at this age, thinking it would make us cooler), two box cutters (something I used at my stock boy position).

My mom screamed out and began sobbing uncontrollably. My dad just stood there, shaking his head in disbelief. Insult to injury. The cop went on and on about how real the pellet gun looked. He asked me if it was loaded. I told him it was not. While talking, he pointed it at the garbage can and pulled the trigger. *Pink!* I heard the pellet hit the inside of the can, then the base. *I'm a dead man! Wait. What is this? He doesn't hear it. He doesn't see it. Nobody does. I'm saved!* A bit more back-and-forth between my parents and the cops before I was released into their custody. No charges were filed against me.

They handed the envelop, with all its contents, back to my parents. As we walked out of the police station, my mother said, "You will never see Tony and Ricky ever again. They are bad influences!"

Seriously? I was the one who stuck the gun out the window. They had no idea what I was going to do. It was their fault? You're crazy. Two takeaways from this story: Tony, Ricky, and I hooked back up less than a week later and remain friends to this day. Forty-eight hours after being released from custody, I found my mother's hiding place for the weapons and stole them back. The buck knife remained in my knife collection (one of my prized possessions), and the pellet gun is in my garage.

*****

Let's move forward to May 1978. Tony secured a primo gig at an electronics store at Six Corners, one of the best shopping areas on the Northwest Side of Chicago. He was a sales associate, selling everything from CB radios (very popular at the time) to high-end stereo systems. Ricky and I visited him every chance we could. We were absolutely in love with the equipment but, even with our part-time jobs, could never afford to buy a unit. The next best thing was to listen to them in the store while Tony was working. I'm sure you know where this is going. It started off simple. Tony stole a few small components for a radio his parents have at home. Next, he decided he wanted to get into the CB radio craze. Out went a unit, followed by an antenna, wiring, etc. Of course, Ricky and I helped him with all this. We visited the store, hung out a bit. He handed us the items, and we placed it in his car truck. All was good. After a few months, Tony was promoted to senior sales associate, giving him access to all the high-end stereo systems. Are they crazy? We didn't complain. We now laid out plans for Ricky and me to take delivery of our stereo systems of choice. I picked out the best Pioneer stereo, turntable, cassette player, and speakers they had in stock. Ricky did the same. This time, we met at the back door and shuttled the big boxes to Tony's car, filling up every available inch. After Tony got off work, he stopped by each of our houses, and we moved the units into our bedrooms. I spent all night setting up my unit. I was familiar with how to operate it after all the hours spent at the stereo store. My parents had no idea I had this system in my room until I cranked it up the next day. No more shitty little turntable with a built-in speaker. This baby, at full power, rattled the bedroom window, along with the rest of the house. My parents went nuts.

"What a waste of money!" (Guess again.) "Turn that crap down!" (Never.)

I was in seventh heaven. Never in a million years did I think I would ever own such an outstanding system. Thank you, Tony! Did we ever feel guilty about stealing these units? Never crossed my mind. At this point, Tony got greedy. He started stealing all kinds of gear and selling it to anyone with a few bucks. Dozens and dozens of units were going out every week. He was flushed with cash and couldn't be happier. Until one day, he was caught heading out the back with a cassette unit. He claimed it was the first time he'd ever took anything and that he was sorry. Not so fast. It turned out the owner of the store noticed a few things were missing and installed cameras throughout the facility. They had hours of tapes showing Tony taking things out the back door. Busted! Tony got arrested. The owner decided to drop the charges if Tony and his parents made restitution. They ended up paying out more than $10K to make things right. As for my stereo? I listened to it every night for the next fifteen years and didn't think twice about it. What a dick I was. Thanks, Tony!

*****

It was the summer of 1978. Life remained grand. At this point in our young lives, we added another variable to the equation—liquor. We discovered, by trial and error, what places in the neighborhood would serve us. By this point, I was able to grow facial hair relatively quickly, which helped even more. I went two to three days without shaving, and I made the rounds. Unlike other kids our age, Ricky and I took a liking to all types of booze, especially hard liquor. The first drink we ever took was not beer. We went straight for the hard stuff. Seagram's Seven to be exact. We loved nothing more than to purchase a half pint or a pint of booze and walk the streets for hours, exploring every nook and cranny of our neighborhood. Our radius, at this point, was in excess of five miles (mind you, without access to a car). In addition to our explorations, we absolutely loved to play tennis. We would play for hours on end. Of course, we had to add a few "changes" to our standard game. Number 1, *everything* was in bounds. We did not limit ourselves to the standard court. As long as the ball made it across the net, it was considered in. The only out-of-bounds we considered was if your shot hit the back fence. Talk about a workout. Man, we covered some ground and, in the process, got ourselves into excellent shape. Not a day would go by where we didn't get a few hours of tennis in. We were pretty obsessed at the time.

The other big change we added to our game was booze. Whenever we played, we always had a cooler full of beer at center court. Between side changes or the completion of a set, we would always pound an ice-cold beer. As they always say, when playing sports, you need to stay hydrated. Most people would recommend water or Gatorade. We preferred Swiss Löwenbräu, Carlsberg Elephant malt liquor, or Pilsner Urquell. Nothing but the good stuff for us. These tennis matches became epic. After a while, all my friends began to join us—Tony, George, Joe, etc. There were many a night where we tied up all three of the courts for hours. By the time we were all done, the whole crew was smoking and joking. Let me tell you, replacing water (sweat) with alcohol makes for the best high in the world! Drinking at this point became a pretty big part of our lives. There was rarely a day in the summer (weekdays as well as weekends) that we did not partake in the festivities. In fact, the time of day didn't matter as well. Case in point. It was eight thirty on a Tuesday morning. I was already at Ricky's house planning out our day. His folks weren't home, so we had the entire place to ourselves. We bantered a few ideas back and forth, but nothing seemed to catch our interest. We finally decided to shoot some pool in his basement until we came up with any better ideas. To make it more interesting, we each decided to grab a pint of Canadian Club from the local White Hen Pantry (a well-known location for selling liquor to minors). We headed out, loaded up, and made our way back to Ricky's.

Just like tennis, we decided to take a swig at the end of each game. Eight, nine, ten games were played. Eight, nine, ten shots were taken. It did not take long until we were completely wasted. The longer we played, the louder and more obnoxious we got—screaming profanities, laughing like little schoolgirls. Suddenly, we got a great idea. How about a little target practice in the basement? We went and grabbed the pellet gun (yes, the same gun used in my earlier story) and loaded that baby up. We then proceeded to flip the oversized couch, on the south wall of the basement, onto its side, exposing the rectangular bottom. We took turns unloading six rounds at a time into the couch. We must have fired off at least seventy-five to one hundred rounds until we got bored of this game. The couch was then flipped over and put back in its proper location. Of course, there were several rounds that had made their way through the front side of the couch.

"No problem, just throw a blanket over the cushion. Your mother will never find out!"

Real brain surgeons, eh? Next on the docket. I was going to make my parents so proud by getting a haircut, something they'd been on my ass to do for months (years?). We stumbled out the back door and somehow, someway, we made it to the barbershop on Belmont Avenue. After several attempts, I was able to get myself situated in the barber's chair. I could barely sit up straight or keep my eyes open. Of course, Ricky and I continued to laugh the entire time, like two escaped mental patients. The barber shook his head as he began to cut my hair. He was about halfway done with the right side of my head when I started feeling a bit sick to my stomach. A few more snips of the hair and I started projectile vomiting into my lap. I had a sheet covering my body, so the vomit rolled off the sheet and shot several feet into the air, eventually covering the mirror, countertop, and equipment directly in front of me. The barber, who could barely speak English, went apeshit. He was screaming, yelling, and throwing his hands in the air. Ricky, being the smooth character that he was, stood up, walked very calmly over to the barber, handed him a $20 bill and said sorry. We exited the shop and made our way north toward home.

About a block before Ricky's house, I decided I was tired and needed to take a nap. Ricky said that was not a bad idea. We proceeded to lay down on the front lawn of one of his neighbors and to pass out. Mind you, this is approximately twelve thirty in the afternoon on a beautiful, sunny day. We woke up in about thirty minutes and decided it was best we go back to our respective homes. We gave each other a big hug (God knows why) and parted company. I was still absolutely loaded. The walk home, which generally took me five minutes, actually turned into a thirty-minute adventure. Every step, every block was an adventure. I finally made it home and somehow made it up to my bedroom. I was covered in puke, so I decided to strip down to my underwear, throw my soiled clothes into the corner (I planned on throwing them away later to help cover the crime), and lie down on my bed. I was only there for five to ten minutes before I started throwing up once again. All over myself. All over the bed.

My older sister was home at the time and hears all the commotion. She bolted into the bedroom and found me in this condition.

She immediately pulled me off my bed, and I hit the floor. *Thump!* I didn't feel a thing. At this point, she sat on my back and started pounding my face on the floor. *Bam, bam, bam!* Again, I didn't feel a thing. The only thing I remember is, I continued to vomit. I can't believe how much food and fluid is being expelled from my body. As I lay on the floor, I saw my stomach contents leaving my mouth, heading across the floor, hitting the back wall, and heading back my way like a tidal wave. The puke rolled back into my face and cascaded over my head and shoulders. I thought it was the coolest thing I'd ever seen. Everything was in slow motion, and I was feeling no pain (even though my sister continued to crack my head against the floor). I finally stopped throwing up and passed out. I woke up several hours later, my head pounding, some ungodly taste in my mouth. I was fully clothed. There was not a spot of puke on my bed, on the floor, anywhere! It was a miracle. Was I dreaming? Just at that moment, my mother came into my room. She asked how I was feeling and if she could get me anything.

"I wonder where you picked up the flu from? I'm going to call your friend's mother and give them a heads-up. You get some rest."

What? Flu? Are you kidding me? I'm in the fucking clear! Outstanding. My sister Karen never spoke a word to me about this incident. It was like it never happened. A few hours later, there was a knock at the front door. It was Ricky. He was stopping by to see how I was holding up. He came upstairs, and we exchanged stories. Turned out he went to work, blasted out of his mind, made it through his shift, and was stopping by to show me some new fishing reels that he happened to "pick up" at work. God bless him. God bless my sister. Isn't life grand? I'd like to tell you I learned my lesson about drinking, but that would be a lie. If anything, we picked up the pace even further going forward. It would take a hell of a lot more than that for us to learn that lesson.

*****

It was now the end of summer, and we were counting down the days for us to head back to school. Ricky and I decided to head out on one last adventure. He knew how much I liked trains (my entire life). We knew of a major railroad yard at Austin and Central, several miles to the south of us. As I mentioned earlier, we did not hesitate to push our boundaries. We didn't think twice about a walk like this. Our original intent was to pick up some beer, head down to the rail yard, and watch the trains go by. We picked up two six-packs of Pilsner Urquell and began our adventure. Again, nothing but the best for us. We got to the rail yard and found a place to sit down to begin drinking. As we talked, we realized that the railcars in front of us were not moving. Five to ten minutes went by and nothing. We decided to take a look inside the cars. As we peered through the holes, we could make out the dark silhouette of a pickup truck. The entire car was full of brand spanking new pickups of all shapes, sizes, and colors. We made our way to the back entrance of the railcar. We jiggled the handle, and it was loose. As we applied more pressure, the handle moved, and the door swung open, revealing the beautiful new trucks. The light bulb went on.

"Why sit on the uncomfortable ground when you can sit in comfort in one of these trucks?"

We made our way up the center of the car, trying each door handle until we found one that opened. We were in! Beers in hand, we slid onto the bench seat of the truck and closed the door. It was dark. It was cool. It was comfortable. A perfect place to sit and drink. We sat and talked for hours. We never once thought about the railroad police. We never once thought what the hell we would do if the train started moving. We just thought how cool it was to be in this situation at that moment. One by one, as we finished our beers, we decided to line them up on the back edge of the bench seat, where the seat matched up with the window. When we were all done, we had twelve empty beer bottles lined up like little soldiers across the back side of the seat. We laughed and joked, thinking how cool it would be when this train pulled into its final destination and the car dealership found our handiwork. To this day, that thought always brings a smile to my face. A sign of the creativity Ricky and I had way back when. What a great way to end our summer!

*****

As we headed into the fall of 1977, we settled back into our routines—school, work, sports, music, drinking, etc. It was a great time to be a teenager. About this time, a few more very important things were being introduced into our lives—drugs and girls. My first interaction with drugs came from my locker mate at school, Lou. We became friends in homeroom, freshman year, and had been locker partners ever since. On one of my days off from work, Lou invited me and another friend of his over to his house after school. We stopped by the local Chinese food restaurant, and each picked up a quart of shrimp fried rice. We headed to his house and huddled in his small dimly lit bedroom. He lit up some incense, just like at Stevie house many years ago. He put on the A side of the Scorpions Love Drive album and cranked it up. He pulled out a small baggie of what appeared to be some type of dry herb. It was pot. From his back pocket, he pulled out a small pipe and loaded it up. He pulled out a lighter, fired it up, took a big drag, and exhaled. The smell of the pot mixed with the smell of the incense. The room was getting hazy. When my turn came, I was a bit apprehensive. Everything we'd been taught about pot in school told us pot led to other hard-core drugs. Fuck it. I took a leap of faith and inhaled. It burned my lungs. I began to cough and wheeze. The other guys chuckled at me, but I continued to smoke. I took another hit. This time it went down much smoother. Hey, this wasn't so bad. This continued for a few minutes. The tunes were cranking, and they sounded great! I dove into my fried rice. It was the best fried rice I had ever eaten. We continued to smoke, eat, and listen to tunes. I was feeling euphoric. This was the best day of my life.

"I love you, guys! Friends forever!"

About an hour later, Lou's mom came crashing through his bedroom door. He was Greek, and his parents spoke very little English. She yelled at him in Greek, and he yelled back at her in a combination of Greek and English. She finally left the room and slammed the door behind her. I was shocked. Didn't she know what the hell we were doing in here? What a cool setup. *Why can't I have parents like that?* A few minutes later, I headed home. As I came into the house and I said hello to my mom, she asked me if I'd been smoking.

"You stink."

Of course, I lied and told her no, that I had only been around others who were smoking.

"That's good. Smoking is very bad for your health. Now get your homework done."

This coming from the woman who smoked through her entire pregnancy with me and popped out a premature baby. Please. I continued to go to Lou's house on a weekly basis. I loved every second of our time together. It doesn't get much better than that!

*****

As for girls, things were really beginning to change. Since the end of grade school, I'd always had a fascination with the opposite sex (as my earlier stories conveyed). I still didn't have a clue what the hell I was supposed to do with them. Ricky was a bit ahead of the game. He actually had a girlfriend the past summer by the name of Laura. I was introduced to her by one of our mutual friends Tony when Ricky left to spend some time at his summer home. He had moved on from her; she was fairly new to the neighborhood and had very few friends. We hit it off immediately. She was a very pretty girl, somewhat shy, but as the months went by, she opened up more and more to me. I was finally getting the inside track on how the mind of a girl worked. I was seriously intrigued. She rapidly became my first real girl *friend* (not girlfriend). We shared everything with each other. A whole new perspective on life. She was now part of my inner circle of friends (Ted, Ricky, Tony, Lou, etc.). Whenever she had a question regarding a certain boy, or vice versa, we were there to answer in great detail. The insight we provided to each other would be invaluable in the coming years.

*****

The balance of 1977 found us doing more of the same as the previous year—more work and more play (drinking, smoking pot, wandering the streets of Chicago, etc.). There are several funny stories I need to share with you from this particular time. They will give you a better idea of the direction my life is heading. One Friday night, Ted and I took a walk to a park south of us called Hansen Park (about a two-mile walk each way). We picked up a twelve-pack of beer and sat back to shoot the shit. As we drank, we got much louder and a whole lot bolder. We were looking for something to do to get out our frustrations. At that moment, we spotted a Chicago police car pull up on a side street closest to us. We were on high alert because we didn't want to get caught drinking. We fell back into the shadows. We noticed the car had pulled up in front of a local tavern. Two policemen exited the vehicle and headed inside. Bar fight? Unruly patron? We stuck around to see what was going down. Fifteen minutes went by. Then thirty. These SOBs weren't there on official duty; they were there to knock a few beers back. Total bullshit! What were we going to do about this situation? The light bulb went off once again.

"Let's go let the air out of their tires!"

We didn't think twice. We sneaked over to where their car was parked. Ted took one side; I took the other. *Hiss…* After about three to four minutes, all four tires were flat. We ran back to our original position to see what happened. Another thirty minutes went by without any movement. This prank was no good unless we see their reaction. We made our way to a local pay phone and called the police. I indicated there was an altercation at Long and Heritage (the corner at which the bar was located) and to come quickly. I slammed the phone down, and we rushed back to our viewing location. Sure as shit, within less than five minutes, two cop cars came screaming up to the bar. All four officers rushed in. A few minutes later, all six cops came out of the bar, scratching their heads. Just then, one of the officers noticed all four tires on their squad car were flat. Every four-letter word in the world was spewing from his mouth. The other officers looked on in disbelief. Ted and I? We were hiding in the shadows (behind a set of bleachers) laughing our ass off! We'd struck a blow for the common man!

*****

One fall evening, Ricky and I were sitting in Chopin Park, once again drinking (beer and Canadian Club this time). After we polished off our liquor, we decided to take a stroll around the neighborhood (as I mentioned earlier, not an uncommon practice for us to partake in after one of our drinking sessions). At the corner of Addison and Central stood the Northwest Community Hospital (about half a mile from Chopin Park). As we were walking by, we noticed a Chicago Police car sitting in the emergency entrance. The light bulb in my head went off once again. No, I was not thinking of flattening their tires this time. I knew they were there to help some poor, innocent soul through some type of issue. No, this time, I had my eye on the top of the car. In the center of the mars lights sat a plastic plate with the assigned patrol car's number. How cool would it be to steal that plate? How many people in the world had such a thing in their possession? (How's that for creativity?)

We made our way across the street. As Ricky stood lookout, I sneaked behind the car, reached onto the roof, slid the plate from its holder, and hauled our ass out of there. We both ran as fast as we could back to the park bench we were sitting on in Chopin Park. Our hearts were racing. The adrenaline was flowing. We did it! I could not believe we had the plate in our hands. We were as high as a kite, reliving the incident over and over until the night was done. I kept the plate with me for safekeeping. We decided this was so cool that we were going to start "collecting" as many of these plates as possible. Over the years, we were able to secure another two or three for the collection. Who else in the city of Chicago could say they had a police car nameplate collection?

*****

As we moved further into the year, we decided to do some cruising in Tony's car. As a reminder, he was a year older than us and actually had his license, as well as access to his father's car. We drove around for hours, looking for something to do. It was a pretty boring night up to this point. As we drove west on Belmont Avenue, we crossed a single set of railroad tracks that ran parallel to the Kimball Candy Company.

"Tony, go back! Let's drive down those tracks!"

Poor Tony. He wanted so much to be part of our clique, to be cool. He was not a drinker, so he felt he needed to win us over with his actions. He made a U-turn and headed back to the tracks. He turned left onto the tracks, and we began heading north toward the candy company. *Bump! Bump! Bump!* We were about two hundred yards off the street when we hit the siding for the candy company. At this point, the tracks we were on went straight while a second set turned off to the building. The first set of tires lurched over the intersecting tracks. Not so fortunate on the back tires. They got wedged between the two sets. Tony panicked and asked us what to do. We were the wrong guys to ask. We told him to gun the engine and that the tires would free themselves. Bad advice. As the car began to accelerate, the overwhelming smell of burning rubber began to fill the car. Tony pushed harder on the gas pedal. More smoke followed by a high-pitched screeching sound. A few more pushes before Tony realized we were stuck. We all jumped out of the car. The tires (brand-new, mind you) had peeled off the back rims just like an apple. A pile of smoking rubber lay beneath the steel rims that were now metal on metal with the tracks. Of course, Ricky and I were laughing at the situation as Tony broke into a low whimper. Neighbors on the side streets parallel to the tracks emerged from their houses. They were shocked to see an automobile on the railroad tracks. Tony wandered over to speak to one of them, then headed into a house to call his father. How would you like to be the one making that call? Not me! He returned after a few minutes to tell us his father, along with a tow truck, were on the way. We sat with the car to await their arrival. I looked at Ricky, and we started laughing again. Tony told us to shut the hell up.

As I stared south down the tracks, I saw a white light in the distance. I figured out early on that the light was stationary. Probably some kind of street light or light hanging off one of the factories down there. Tony didn't know that. The devil horns popped out of my skull as I screamed out, "Train!" Tony looked south and went into pure panic mode. He jumped back into the car and started hammering on the gas pedal again. The sound of grinding metal was almost too much to handle. After a few minutes of that, he went to plan B. He went to the rear of the car and started pushing. He screamed at us to do the same. There was no way in God's greater earth we were going to move this car. It was a monstrous Buick Electra, weighing almost five thousand pounds. I looked back and said the light appeared to be getting closer (lying SOB). Tony was crying uncontrollably. I stood there with the biggest smirk on my face. I said it was best we move to the side for if/when the train arrived.

Just then, Tony's father arrived with the tow truck. He was a small guy but was a real-ass kicker. He jumped out and was immediately screaming at Tony. He made his way up the siding, grabbed Tony by the ear, and pulled him down toward the car. The tow truck driver hooked up a cable to the back of the car and started dragging it off to the side street. All we heard was metal cracking; all we could see were pieces of the car flying off in all directions. The rims sheared off. The back panels were crushed. The car was a total mess. When the show was over, Tony (still crying, father still screaming) was dragged into his father's other car and whisked away. Poor guy. Ricky and me? We shrugged our shoulders and set out on the two-mile walk home. Just another day in our crazy lives. No guilt. No remorse. It was not our fault he listened to us!

*****

It was now the fall of 1977, and I was entering into my sophomore year of high school. Life was great! Another year, another opportunity for me to get back into drug use with Lou (locker partner) and his friends. We continued to listen to heavy metal. The harder and faster, the better. We all fell in love with a group called UFO from England. They had a guitar player, Michael Schenker, who was absolutely off the charts! It just so happened they were coming to Chicago in October. We all agreed that we *must* attend this show. We rushed out and bought tickets as close to the stage as possible. As the date got closer, the realization of how we were going to get there settled in. They were playing at the International Amphitheater on the Southwest Side of Chicago, miles and miles from our home. By this point in my life, I had ridden both the buses and the EL, but mostly on easy, straight shots. I had *never* ventured this far away from home. I picked up a route booklet from one of the local bus drivers. I brought it to our next session, and we laid out our plans. We were going to have to take three different buses, through several very bad neighborhoods, to reach our final destination. We didn't care. It was worth putting our lives on the line to see these guys.

The day arrived, and we headed out on our little adventure. Surprisingly, the ride was uneventful, and we made it there in one piece. As we entered the IA, we were blown away by its size. Many years ago, it was used for livestock shows. The walls were massive; the ceiling many stories above us. There was music cranking over the speakers. People everywhere. Prior to the start of the show, a man came on the loud speaker and told us the band would be recording this session for a possible *live* album.

"Please make your presence known!"

The place went crazy. A few minutes later, the lights went down, and the band began to play. Between the music blasting and the fans screaming, my ears were ringing. I could feel the power and energy pounding off my chest. I was screaming so loud my vocal cords were straining and my throat was sore. I didn't give a shit! This was the coolest thing I had ever seen or been part of in my short, little life. I was awestruck. I never wanted to stop. About halfway through the show, the lead singer indicated that this was their last show on this tour and that we could basically tear the place down once they were done playing. Are you kidding me? We took it up another level. My whole body was vibrating; my mind was running wild in anticipation of the show coming to an end. After two encores, the lights came up, and the place went nuts. Kids climbed onto the stage and started tearing things apart. Shit was flying everywhere—two-by-fours, chairs, bottles, you name it. It was a total free for all. Of course, we participated. We loved it! After about thirty minutes of just pure craziness, people started filing out of the theater. It was about midnight as we made our way to the bus stop for the long journey home. This would be a night I would never forget. I was hooked on live rock/metal music for the rest of my life. Going to as many concerts as I could became a top priority (Aerosmith, Thin Lizzy, Ted Nugent, etc.). I couldn't get enough! This is true, even to this day.

*****

Shortly after this adventure, Tony decided to have a party at his house. Tony's parents were gone for the weekend, so he invited a few close friends over. Of course, his parents told him no parties, but who listens to that? Besides, he was going to keep it low-key. Sandwiches, chips, pop, music, and games were all on the agenda. What could possibly go wrong? For starters, you invited me. What was wrong with me inviting a few more friends? What was wrong with some booze? What was wrong with a little pot? What started out being a low-key party for a dozen or so people turned into a madhouse. There were now forty to fifty people at the house—inside, outside, and in every room in the house. People kept coming. There was booze everywhere. People were dropping food and alcohol all over his parents' beautiful home (furniture, carpet, bedspreads, etc.). It was totally out of control, and there was not a damn thing in the world Tony could do.

We set up a bong in Tony's garage. We all sat crossed-legged on the concrete floor and took our turns. There was so much smoke pouring out it looked like the garage was on fire. Every light was on in the house. There were kids everywhere, metal music pouring out of the stereo speakers. I remained in the garage. Beer in both hands as I awaited my turn. Suddenly, the light went on, and the garage door opened. What the hell was going on? Who the hell did that? The door fully opened to reveal car headlights beginning to turn into the garage. The car came to a stop in the alley, and two bodies emerged. It was Tony's parents! They were home early! Holy shit! We all began to run out in all directions, like rats scurrying off a sinking ship. I bolted for the house to tell Tony. He was sitting in the corner of the living room, his face flush, tears streaming down his face. He knew he'd lost complete control of his home, and there was not a damn thing he could do. I alerted him of his parents' arrival, and he looked like he'd seen a ghost. He bolted up from his chair and headed to the back of the house. Over the blare of the music, I heard some very loud screaming. Tony's father had made his entrance and was, once again, pulling Tony around by his ear. People started exiting. The extent of the damage was becoming quite clear.

I said hello to Tony's father (just being polite), but he looked right past me. He was in a rage and rightfully so. I waved goodbye to Tony and headed out the back door. "Poor guy," I said to myself. "Great party." And I headed home. Not once did I take responsibility in my mind for what just transpired. Selfish? Self-centered? I don't think so.

*****

It was about this time I got my first girlfriend. Her name was Diedra. She was the oldest daughter of my mom's best friend. I'd seen her numerous times in the past but never had the guts to ask her out. As I got older and my self-confidence grew, I finally worked up enough guts to ask her out. I was shocked when she said yes. On our first date, I took her to dinner and a movie. We had to walk there and back as I had no license or a car. She was cool with that. Upon arrival back to her house, I fumblefucked around with my goodbye. I knew this was the time you should kiss and leave, but I didn't know what the hell I was doing. Finally, she pulled my head toward her and thrust her tongue into my mouth. What the fuck? I'd kissed several girls in the past but never like this. I moved my tongue around like I knew what the hell I was doing. After a few minutes, she stopped, gave me a smile, and said good night. All the way home, I was thinking about what just transpired. My initial fright had now turned into thoughts of happiness, even arousal. Whatever that was, I wanted more of it. We went on a few more dates. We were very comfortable with each other. I finally figured out what we were doing was called French-kissing, and I couldn't get enough of it. Every time I dropped her off, we got right down to it. Two minutes now turned into twenty minutes. Life was good. We continued to see each other for several months. I never wanted it to end. Of course, being the dumbass that I was, it didn't take long before I blew it.

I was at the park one day with my friends. The topic of girls came up (as it did more and more these days). Everybody was going around the horn, sharing their escapades. I got caught up in the moment. I told my buds I'd been all over Diedra. I got into some fairly graphic details about what we'd been up to. Of course, they were all lies. I just mastered French-kissing. I didn't know my ass from a hole in the ground when it came to second or third base. Unfortunately, one of my friends' mothers was also friends with Diedra's mother. This idiot went home and told his mother what I said, and she, in turn, proceeded to call Diedra's mother. It didn't take long before she was on the phone with my mother.

"Bob, get your ass down here immediately!" She proceeded to tell me what was said and read me the riot act. "You are to get on the phone and apologize to the young lady about all the garbage you said about her!"

Busted. I reluctantly picked up the phone, and her mother picked up. "May I please speak to Diedra?" She knew it was me. She handed off the phone.

"Hello?"

Holding back tears, I proceeded to apologize to her for all the lies I told. She seemed very forgiving. "Are we still good after all this?" I asked her if we could go out on a date this coming Friday. *Slam!* The phone went dead. I took that as a resounding *no*. Such was the story about my first girlfriend.

*****

It was now late fall of 1977. My friendship with Laura continued to blossom. She was pulled further into my inner circle of friends. There was nothing I wouldn't do for her (as was the case with all my good friends). Earlier in the year, she told me a story about a neighbor boy across the street who had been harassing her. Nothing of significance, but I put him on my radar just the same. Shortly after she told me this story, a wicker chair got stolen from the front porch of her house. Of course, I immediately came to the conclusion that Henry (the boy across the street) did it. *Fuck that! I'll show him what happens when you fuck with one of my inner-circle friends.* Step 1, I took a gallon of black paint from my parents' basement. Henry parked his car on the street in front of his house. Ricky and I headed over there one night and repainted Henry's car from bright yellow to full-on black. The entire body, windows, and chrome included were covered in paint. That would show him! We were not done yet. For the past several months, Ricky and I had been messing around with firecrackers. We bored of the usual light and throw. Not enough action. Not enough bang for the buck. We experimented with making our own "devices." We removed the gunpowder from the firecrackers and placed it in any type of metal canister we could find. Today you would probably call these a form of pipe bombs. We settled on metal canisters that you store film in that keep it from getting exposed. We built a unit in his basement. We removed the screw-on cap from the cylinder. We filled the cylinder with powder. We punched a hole in the top of the canister. We inserted a wick into the hole (a wick we pulled out of an M-80 earlier in the day). We screwed down the cap as tightly as we could. Ready for action! We headed down the alley behind Henry's house. We walked back and forth, scoping out our target. We settled on his garage door. On our last pass by, I placed the device on the garage door handle, lit the fuse, and we both ran like hell. *Bam!*

As we turned the corner, the sound reverberated off the other garages. We hauled ass all the way back to Ricky's house. We lay low for a few hours. We couldn't hold back our excitement. We had to go and see what our handiwork had resulted in. We headed back out (nighttime) and over to Henry's alley. As we walked by, we saw the massive destruction we had caused. The explosion blew a hole in the door the size of a pie plate. The garage door was off its track and hanging on by a thread. Success! We were blown away (no pun intended) by the damage we had caused. *That will show you who's boss!* Of course, we had no proof that Henry was responsible for the missing chair. We didn't care. Somebody must be punished. Why not Henry and his family? Blaze on!

*****

1978–1979

The winter of 1978 brought a series of significant changes to my core group of friends. First, Ted, my best friend at St. Pat's, informed me that his parents had bought a house in the western suburbs and they would be moving at the end of the school year. He was going to finish out the year here and transfer to a different school in the fall. I was devastated. We did everything in school together. We were in the same classes. We ate lunch together. We skipped school and played hooky together. *What the hell am I going to do next year?* Second, my very best friend in the whole world, Ricky, had been expelled from his high school. He'd been caught up in some type of drug activity. From what I could gather, he was in the wrong place at the wrong time. Regardless of the circumstances, he was no longer a student at Holy Cross High School. Based on the time of year this situation occurred, he was left with no choice but to attend Foreman, our local public high school. Let me tell you, after spending the last ten-plus years in the Catholic education system, the last thing you want to do is spend any amount of time at Foreman. Unfortunately, he was left with no choice but to spend the balance of his sophomore year in a school full of gangsters, potheads, and delinquents. I was worried for him, but there was not much I could do. I tried to spend as much time as I could with him (after school) to keep his spirits up. Finally, Laura told me she'd hooked up with an old schoolmate from her previous neighborhood and was in *love*. I found out early on that love meant you spend every second of every waking day together. They were inseparable for the first three months together. Ted was leaving. Ricky was in a bad place. Laura had said goodbye to all her friends, including me. It was a strange time, but I learned to adapt.

*****

Thankfully, in early spring, Laura brought her boyfriend around to meet me. His name was Larry. He was a few years older than us and, at the time, appeared to be so much wiser and cooler. The more I got to know him, the more I began to like him. Laura, Larry, and I started to spend quite a bit of time together. Whenever and wherever that was, booze was always in the picture. We quickly established two places as our favorite hangout. The first was a smoke-laden pool hall at Diversey and Central (about one mile from my house). It was a small storefront with blackened windows, a purple neon sign that said Pool above the front entrance. As far as I know, it had no name. As you walk into the haze, there was a counter on the left-hand side. This was where you pick up your balls and rack. Straight ahead and to the right, there were fifteen to twenty regulation-sized pool tables. You scan the area and pick your table of choice. We tried to find a table far enough away from the creep balls (a hard thing to do based on the fact that majority of the people in there were creep balls) and set up shop. At first, we all sucked. As time passed, we got better and better. The real bonus was, you could drink beer and shoot pool all night. Nobody ever checked our identification. Nobody ever questioned us. It didn't take long before we became one of the regulars. We were, by far, the youngest people in the joint. We didn't care; this was cool stuff. We felt like big boys and girls.

The second place of choice was called Central Gyros. It was exactly a half mile from the pool hall as you made your way toward home. It was a very small Greek restaurant, no more than six dimly lit booths to choose from. We heard through the grapevine that gyro meat was to die for. One day, heading back from the pool hall, we decided to give it a go. We all agreed it was outstanding and that we needed to come back soon. On our second visit, we got brave.

"Three gyros and a pitcher of Miller please!"

Within five minutes, we had food and drink in front of us. Nobody ever check our identification or asked our age. Let me tell you something, there is nothing better than gyros and beer! Not a week went by where we didn't hit Central Gyros. The only thing that changed over the years was the amount of beer that we consumed. We went from one pitcher per visit to numerous pitchers as the months progressed. Nine times out of ten, we staggered out of the place, rip-roaring drunk. What fun! By this point in my life, coming home drunk was a fairly standard occurrence. Every time I walked through the door, my parents would ask to smell my breath.

"*Bbbllaahhh!*" Of course, I smelled like a brewery/distillery every time.

*****

"You've been drinking! Upstairs, mister. You are hereby grounded for a week, month, whatever..."

Of course, the groundings never stuck. I was back at it the following week. Every weekend was like Groundhog Day. One time, my parents warned me that if I came home late and drunk, they were going to lock me out of the house. True to their word, I got home one Friday morning at about one thirty. The front and back doors were locked. The house was completely dark. What my parents expected (I know them very well by now) was that I would ring the bell, then they would let me in and proceed to read me the riot act. Fuck that! Larry was still with me at this point. Initially, we decided to lay down and sleep on one of the park benches across the street from my house. The light bulb went off at this point. Going back to my paper delivery days, I remembered that the majority of the multiunit apartment complexes had heated entryways.

"Why don't we go and sleep in one of those? I know the perfect spot."

We walked about two blocks west to the corner of Roscoe and Central. We headed to the first entrance on the right side of the complex. It was well lit and warm. Larry and I curled up in opposite corners, using old newspapers for a pillow. We were both out like a light in five minutes. Fast-forward to about 6:00 a.m. that same morning. I sensed someone was looking down on me. As my eyes opened and came into focus, there was an old man kneeling in front of me, about six inches from my face. He was nudging me with his right arm as he held his left hand on my forehead.

"Are you okay? I thought you were dead."

I shuffled to my feet. The smell of vomit filled my nose. Apparently, sometime in the morning hours, I puked up all the gyros and beer from the previous night. It was spread out across the floor. It was all over my clothes, in my hair, stuck to my face, etc. I shook the old man's hand (transferring a bit of dried-up gyros in the process) and headed for home. As I headed up the stairs of my house, my mom swung the door open and began to yell.

"Where in the hell have you been, young man? My god, look at yourself!"

I was still buzzed. "You're the one who locked your son out of his house" was my reply. Smart-ass. With my mom screaming in my ear, I headed directly to the bathroom to strip my puke-laden clothes off and take a shower. Upon my exiting the bathroom, my mom informed me that I was grounded for a month. I smiled, chuckled a bit, and headed upstairs to pass out for the next ten hours. To say I was getting a bit out of control would be the understatement of the year.

*****

The summer of 1978 found me hooking up with my next girlfriend. Her name was Stephanie. She went to the same grade school as me and was a year younger than me. She was a very pretty brunette with rosy cheeks and a beautiful body. We went on a few dates (Cubs game, local carnival, etc.) and hung out together as often as we could. She rapidly became part of the Laura, Larry, and Bob clique. On a very hot day in June, the four of us decided to head down to the beach. We packed a bag of snacks and booze and jumped on the Belmont Avenue bus heading east toward the lake. We were looking forward to lying out, catching some rays, and having a few drinks. It was approximately 10:00 a.m. when we reached our destination. Of course, being the tough guys that we were, we immediately tapped into the fifth of Jack Daniels. By noon, we were absolutely plastered. Time for a swim. Stephanie and I headed into the surf. We jumped around, hugging and kissing each other. It doesn't get any better than this.

Suddenly, as Stephanie got a bit deeper, the top of her suit fell off. She was so drunk she had no idea what was happening. She continued to jump and laugh as I desperately tried to pull her top up. I myself was wasted, and even this simplest of task was difficult for me to complete. After about ten minutes passed, I decided the best thing to do was get her back on our beach towels and straighten this situation out. Top still down, Stephanie jumped on my back for a piggyback ride. I got her to the shore and laid her down on our beach towels. Instead of covering her up immediately, I decided now was the time to land a big old hickey on her right breast. Job completed. Maybe just one more. And another. This went on for at least thirty minutes. I eventually tired of this activity and proceeded to pass out. Mind you, it was a beautiful summer day, and the beach was quite crowded. God knows how many people had seen this spectacle. It was absolutely amazing that nobody told us to stop or that we did not get arrested for a lewd act in a public place. It was now 3:00 p.m., and we had all woken up from our slumber. We were still high as kites as we made our way to the bus stop. Not a word was spoken among us. We boarded the Belmont Avenue bus heading westward toward home. I closed my eyes to give them a rest. Next thing I know, I was being shaken violently by the bus driver.

"End of the line, pal! Up and at 'em!"

As my eyes came into focus, I saw the rest of my crew slouched over in their seats. We had slept past our stop and were in the bus turn-around at Belmont and Cumberland. As I woke everyone else, I begged the driver to please let us stay on the eastbound bus until we get home. He took pity on us and agreed. As we exited the bus at Belmont and Long, we all headed off in different directions. Every man and woman for themselves. I went home and, once again, passed out. I awoke about 8:00 p.m. and made my way over to Stephanie's house. I wanted to check on her to make sure she made it home okay. What a gentleman, eh? (A real gentleman would have walked her home from the bus stop). She let me in and took me to her bedroom. She was still feeling the ill effects from the JD. Her parents thought she had the flu (been there, done that!). She proceeded to ask me if I remembered what happened that day.

"I remember some, but most of the day is a blur."

She proceeded to roll down part of her T-shirt to reveal the upper part of her breast. It was covered with red marks from top to bottom. She rolled down the other side to reveal the same condition. It looked like some kind of wild animal did a number on her. After searching my mind for some kind of explanation, it became quite evident that wild animal was me. What a piece of shit. This became one of many times that I swore to myself I would never drink again! How could I have done such a terrible thing to some innocent girl? I felt terrible. Needless to say, as time passed, so did my relationship with Stephanie. We were never really able to get past this situation. Wherever you are, Stephanie, I hope you will forgive me!

*****

The end of summer was rapidly approaching. It was August of 1978, and I was preparing for my junior year at St. Pat's. A bit earlier in the month, I received some great news from Ricky. He would be transferring from Foreman to St. Patrick's for the balance of his high school career. With Ted's departure, the timing couldn't be better! I got to spend the balance of my time in high school with my best friend in the world. I was flying high. Unfortunately, the high did not last long. Two weeks prior to me starting school, my dad pulled me aside to have a heart to heart. He informed me that his business was failing and that money was very, very tight right now.

"With your older sister, Karen, heading into her senior year at Notre Dame, I have an obligation to pay her tuition. That being said, I will not have enough money to pay for your tuition at St. Pat's. I'm so very sorry. Of course, you have choices. You can transfer to Foreman to finish out your last two years of high school, or you can find some way to pay your own tuition at St. Pat's. Again, I'm so sorry. I wish I had better news for you."

What did he just say? Did I hear him correctly? Foreman High School? No more St. Pat's? My head started spinning. Everything was going dark. I began to cry, light at first, increasing to a full-on bawl. What the hell was I going to do? I felt like swan diving off the roof. I went to my room and continued to cry for what seemed like hours. I continued to run both scenarios through my head. Once again, that light bulb went off in my head. *Wait a minute, I have thousands of dollars in my Colonial Bank savings account. Certainly more than I will need to pay my tuition.* Disaster averted!

First, I called St. Pat's to find out what my monthly tuition bills would be. Once I had that figured out, I headed down to the bank to reconfirm my balance. *I've got this covered!* I handed my bankbook to the teller and asked her to please update it accordingly. She went to a cabinet directly behind her station. She pulled out an index card from the bin and compared it to my bankbook. She looked at one, then the other, for the next five minutes. When she was done, she called a gentleman in a blue suit over to the cabinet. They talked in whispers.

I was thinking, *What the hell is going on? Just give me my number, and I'll be on my way.*

She slipped the card back into the cabinet, and she and blue suit made their way back to my window.

"Young man, do you know who Emil Sorensen is?"

I stated, "Of course, I do. He's my father."

"I'm sorry to inform you, your account has been closed out by your father. You know longer have any funds at this bank."

"What did you just say? There must be a mistake. I've had an account here since I was born. Every birthday check, graduation gift, every penny earned from the jobs I've worked over the years, paper routes through my current job at Johnson, etc. have been deposited into this bank account." I asked them to check again. They reconfirmed the account had been closed. I stumbled out of the bank. I was in a blur. I was confused. I was angry. I was scared. I immediately headed home to confront my father. I was still holding out hope that there was some kind of explanation and that my money was somewhere. He proceeded to tell me, as he did earlier, that it had been a rough year for him and that he needed to use that money to pay our bills. It was a matter of survival. He went on to say if it was any consolation, he had to do the same with my sisters' accounts as well. Consolation? Are you kidding me? All my sisters had in their accounts were a few hundred dollars they received to date for their birthdays and such. I had thousands upon thousands of dollars in my account. I was crushed! I was devastated! What the hell was I going to do now? School would start in a few weeks, and I didn't have a dime to my name. Going to Foreman was not an option!

After another crying jag, I realized I only had one option. I needed to get as many hours as I could at Johnson Drugs so I could pay my tuition and finish my career out at St. Pat's. I immediately headed down to Johnson and talked to my boss. I told him about my situation, and he was shocked but very understanding. As it turned out, the store was very busy, and he could most certainly give me more hours, as many as I could handle. Goodbye sports. Goodbye social life. It was time to be a big boy and make a living. Talk about a shock to the system.

It was 1978. I was going into my junior year of high school. I was forced to grow up in a hurry if I wanted to maintain my existing lifestyle. As of September 1, 1978, I began working full-time at Johnson Drugs—Monday through Friday, 2:00 p.m. to 9:00 p.m., and Saturday, 9:00 a.m. to 2:00 p.m. Of course, I could work more hours if I liked. The balance of Saturday. All day Sunday. Whatever I could handle. My life became school, work, homework, and sleep. Very little time for anything else. I became like a robot, just walking through life. Everything had changed in an instant, and I was forced to accept this new reality or lie down and die. Needless to say, I pressed on!

*****

1978–1979

To say I was angry at how things turned out was the understatement of a lifetime. I went from a happy, carefree life to one of immense stress and pressure. I was forced to become an adult before my time. The balance of my childhood (teenage years) had been torn away from me at an instant. I must find a way to keep my grades up. I must find the energy to go to school all day and work a full-time job at night. I must find the time in between all this to complete my homework assignments. It was not easy. Somehow, I found the strength and structure to make it happen. Did I have much of a choice? After working at Johnson for well over a year now, combined with my full-time status (and additional responsibility), the store manager decided to give me my own set of keys to the door—front, back door, alarm system, even the key to the pharmacy. He believed I was old enough and mature enough for this huge responsibility. I was so honored. My head swelled with pride. A grown-up actually trusted me enough to give me the key to the store!

"Thank you, John. I won't let you down!"

For the first thirty days, I was the employee of the month. I worked like a wild man, trying to do everything better and faster than any adult on staff. I was unloading trucks. I was stocking shelves. I was keeping the whole store looking presentable. My boss could not be happier. I was able to keep up with my studies, but at this point, my job became the most important thing in my life. It was where I get most satisfaction out of life. People didn't treat me like an immature kid. I was an adult just like them. We were friends no matter what the age difference was. It didn't get any better than this. Unfortunately, my adultlike behavior did not last long. Mind you, I was still a junior in high school. I was still attracted to the things I enjoyed doing before being thrust into adulthood. The number 1 thing I'd always enjoyed doing with my friends was drinking. It just so happened that Johnson Drugs had their own rather impressive liquor department. The other thing I'd enjoyed doing throughout my life was stealing. Why pay for something when you could get it for free? Do you see where I'm going with this? Alcohol plus keys to the store equates to free booze.

*****

Starting with the coming Friday evening, I made arrangements for Ricky to meet me at the back door at a set time. Five minutes prior, I grabbed a fifth of CC from the back storage room and awaited his arrival. I swung the door open, and there he was. The handoff was made, Ricky disappeared into the shadows, and I locked the door. I went back to my duties, nobody the wiser. As always, I was not caught. What a beautiful thing! The store closed at nine, and I proceeded to walk to Chopin Park to join back up with Ricky. He was waiting on a park bench at the far north side of the park. As I got closer, we were smiling from ear to ear. Our smiles turned into laughter as he cracked open the bottle, and we began to drink. It was going to be a good night. This rapidly became our Friday and Saturday night ritual. Seeing the booze was free, we began broadening our horizons. There was nothing we wouldn't try at least once—bourbon, scotch, gin, tequila, wine, tons of beer. We refined our tastes and reduced the list of choices down to "nothing but the finest." Our system was working out so well we decide to pick up the pace on how often we steal.

At this point, I don't think there was a day that went by without us taking something out of the store. The problem we were faced with was, where we would keep the stuff. We were able to sneak a few things into our rooms (I actually stored mine in the gutters outside my bedroom window), but there was just too much to do that with. As luck would have it, we found an all-brick garage with the roof partially caved in from the heavy snows last year. The side door was locked, but we found a way to crawl through a small hole on the west wall of the unit. There was enough light coming through the filthy windows in the back that we could maneuver around quite easily.

There was an old rack pushed up against the east wall. It was full of car parts, oil cans, bug spray, etc. We cleaned off the entire unit and began setting up shop. Within two to three weeks, we had our own little liquor store set up in the garage. How pretty that looked! How exciting it was! Whenever we were running low on anything, it was off to our liquor store to load up and party.

As the weeks went by, our stock grew tenfold. We couldn't stop stealing. We couldn't stop replenishing. The garage would serve its purpose for the balance of our high school years. We would even turn our friends onto it. We gave them the okay to grab whatever they wanted as long as they did not get caught going in or out. It was a perfect setup, until one day, in the winter of 1980. I shuffled a few cases out the back door to where Ricky was waiting. Seeing it was five minutes to nine (closing time), I told him to wait for me out back, and we'd head down to our "store" together. As we made our way down the back alley, we were debating back and forth about our booze of choice for the evening. As we neared our destination, something looked wrong. As we reached our destination, something was definitely wrong. The garage was gone! All that was left was a discolored concrete slab. No sign of our stock anywhere. We stood and stared in disbelief. We were both speechless. I felt a tear welling up in my left eye. After what seemed like an hour, we shrugged our shoulders and made the executive decision that it was time to drink some beer. We'd figure all this out later.

*****

Back to 1979 at Johnson. I continued to work hard and thoroughly enjoyed my job. Unfortunately, the whole stealing thing got taken to a whole other level. Two significant things happened that contributed to this situation. First, I found out all the cashiers (the older woman) were doing a bit of stealing of their own (cigarettes, makeup, alcohol, etc.). They were taking things right out the front door. At the time, management trusted us, and there was never anyone checking bags on the way out. Seeing they were doing it, why wouldn't I get into the mix? I would come to my job right after school. I had a white cloth bag, with a set of pull strings, that I would load my books into and sling over my shoulder for the walk home. It became a perfect thing to take stuff out of the store in. Never any booze. Just anything and everything I ever needed at the time. School supplies, food, clothes, magazines—you name it, I stole it. Second, I spread the word around school that I could get anyone any kind of booze they desired at an extremely low price. It did not take long before the word got around. It started out slow. A few guys approached me with their orders. I set up a time to meet them at the back door, and the exchange was made. They were happy because they'd gotten their booze for the evening. I was happy because I'd gotten more cash in my pocket. A real win-win!

Things picked up quite a bit as the weeks progressed. I couldn't keep all the orders straight. I got myself a spiral notebook. During the week, I started writing down the names and orders. I established a price and a set pickup time for each. Upon arrival to work Friday afternoon, I started pulling my orders. By Friday evening (7:00 p.m.), I had a line of cars (and some foot traffic) stretching around the building. Open door. Cash provided. Booze handed off. Close door.

Repeat. This could go on for over an hour. It was not uncommon to complete twenty to thirty transactions a night. Of course, this did not include my core friends. I also took great care of them. I never took a penny from any of them. As if this wasn't enough, I also took delivery orders. Guys would tell me what they wanted, and I would hand it off to them at school the next day. That's right, school—St. Patrick's High School for boys. I would load the booze into my book bag and "clink" my way down the hallway. Upon arrival at my locker, I would actually line up the bottles on the top shelf and make the exchanges throughout the day.

It gets better. Lou, my locker partner and good buddy, was heavy into drug at this time. In addition to pot, he would sell speed, LCD, etc. to anyone and everyone. He would also store his goodies in our locker. Top shelf was booze. Bottom shelf was drugs. We ran this business out our locker for two years and *never* got caught. They had random locker checks that we never fell victim to. The fun thing was, we were never very discrete about what we were doing. We'd do a very half-assed job of trying to cover up what we were handing off. Totally out of control! We were invincible!

Back to Johnson. As the months progressed, so did the thefts. Shit was going out the front door. Shit was going out the back door. My pockets were bulging with cash. This, combined with the legit money I was earning, made me a very rich man. Paying my tuition was a walk in the park. I was so flushed with cash I couldn't spend it fast enough. I kept a small box in my closet that was stuffed full of tens and twenties. If I wanted some new clothes, I bought them. If I wanted to eat out at even the fanciest of restaurants, I did it. Nothing was out of reach for me.

*****

It was now the summer of 1979. Things were going along smoothly, not a care in the world. At the time, I was working with an older gentleman named Al. He and I got along just great. He'd been part of the theft ring since day 1. No big deal. Everyone did it. Al had a beautiful 1972 green metallic Chevelle, black vinyl top, black racing stripes, Cragar rims. It was the kind of car a kid my age could only dream about. Part of my job was to take his car, drive to the bank to get some change (rolls of quarters, dimes, nickels, etc.), and head back to the store. By now, I had my driver's license, but no access to a vehicle. With the amount of drinking I was doing at the time, there was no way in God's greater earth my parents were going to give me access to their car. This was my only opportunity to drive, and I loved every second of it. Especially in such a cool car! Upon his arrival, Al would put his car keys on the peg hook next to the entryway door to the store. When I needed to go to the bank, I would just grab the keys and go. We had and understanding.

It was early June, and Al and I were talking. He had a party coming up, and he needed some booze. He asked me to grab a box and fill it with the items on his list. A liquor box generally held twelve bottles. I noticed he was about three to four bottles short of a full case.

"Would you mind taking out these items for me and we can catch up later?"

Of course, he had no problem with that. I filled the box and placed it by the back door. Ten minutes later, Al opened the back door and walked the case out to his car. As he was opening his trunk, the store manager confronted him. Busted! What did he do next? He started ratting out everyone in the store, including me. When confronted of course, I denied everything.

"I have no idea what he's talking about. I'm just a kid. Besides, I don't drink." I lied, lied, lied like a rug. The manager didn't know what to think about the situation. In his eyes, I'd been a good kid and a hard worker. He floated the idea about me taking a lie detector test. I told my parents, and they went nuts. They headed to the store and informed my manager, "No child of mine is ever going to take a lie detector test! Not in my lifetime! He will quit before that happens!" The manager backed off immediately. He then went on to tell them what a great kid I was and what a wonderful example I was to kids of my age.

Seriously? I thought to myself. I was going to get away with this shit once again. Scot-free. I couldn't believe it. I was reinstated and back to work like nothing happened. Within a week's time, the cars were wrapped around the building, and I was back in business. The one thing that was bugging me was Al. Why would he try to take me down with him? I thought he was my friend. My inquisitiveness turned to anger. *How dare he do this to me! Doesn't he know I need this job?* I didn't think about him, his wife, his two kids. It was strictly about little old me and how he was trying to impact my little world. As I was sweeping the back dock, that damn old light bulb went off in my head once again. *Could it be possible the keys to his car are still on that hook?* I dropped my broom and ran to the doorway. Yes, they were! Outstanding. I grabbed the keys and put them in my pocket. I had no idea what I was going to do at this point, just that I had the keys. This upcoming weekend, Ted was coming back to the neighborhood for a visit. Of course, we were going to hook up, catch up on things, and do some drinking. It was Saturday night, and we were drinking some beer at Chopin Park. I told him about my near miss at Johnson. I told him about what Al tried to do to me. The more we drank, the angrier I got. I was not sure whose idea it was, but between the two of us, we decided the best thing to do was to steal his car. We hid the rest of the beer in some bushes (for consumption later) and headed out to Al's house. He lives a few blocks from Hanson Park, the same place Ted and I let the air out of the police car several years ago. We reached his house, and as luck would have it, that beautiful Chevelle was sitting outside the front door of his home. Without even a second thought, we headed straight for the car. I unlocked the driver's side door and slid in behind the wheel. I reached over and let Ted in. I put the key in the ignition, turned the engine over, and away we go!

I was drunk. I only had a few hours behind the wheel of a car at this point. It was dark. I didn't even have my wallet (license). I didn't give a shit. As we drove around, I came up with another idea. It was not just good enough we stole his car. No. We needed to take it up a notch. We needed to destroy it. Really teach him a lesson. I headed over to Hanson Park, over the curb, and proceeded to drive approximately a quarter mile into the center of the park. We hopped out. We opened both doors, the truck, and the hood. With both hands, we started tearing anything and everything we could out of the car. I pulled out two box cutters from my back pockets—one for Ted, one for me. The items that we couldn't tear out, we cut to shreds. Every seat. Every hose. Every belt. Ted found a brink somewhere. He was now bashing out every window, the taillights, the headlights. This frenzied activity went on for about thirty minutes. We tired. One more swift kick to the side panel and I was done. I took the keys and threw them down a sewer.

"That will teach you to fuck with me!"

I was so damn proud of myself. In my pea brain, it was an eye for an eye. If that wasn't the definition of "youth gone wild," then I have no idea what is.

*****

Earlier in the year, I met another girl named Kathy. She was another of Ricky's girlfriends whom he had since cast away. For some odd reason, I did not meet her through Ricky. He was pretty private when it came to his girlfriends. I actually met her through a mutual friend. Just like Laura, we developed a very tight bond very early on and we confided in each other about everything. For whatever reason, it was so much easier to share your most private thoughts with a girl rather than your buddies. They were nonjudgmental and always told you the truth. Quickly, Kathy was added to my inner circle of friends. Shortly after meeting her, she invited me to join her at the Cubs game with two of her friends from school. Three girls, one guy. Are you kidding me? I was in. She and I jumped on the eastbound Addison bus. Two stops up and her friends Geri and Nancy joined us. We all began to talk. They were both pleasant and pretty. Nancy, in particular, caught my eye. She was a beautiful girl, dark-brown hair, brown eyes, a beautiful body. As the day progressed, I found out what a real Cubs fan she was. In fact, what a real sports fan she was. Are you kidding me? Smart, pretty, athletic, loves sports, etc. I was about to jump out of my skin.

I didn't waste time. On the bus ride home, I asked her out on a date, and she said yes. I could not believe my luck. We went on a few dates and hit it off big-time. What a great fit! There was nothing I didn't like about this girl. Within a month, we decided to go steady. I saw her every weekend. My drinking and gallivanting must be put on the back burner (don't worry, I certainly find time to partake in between my time with Nancy). She lived at Foster and Central. To see her, I must jump on the northbound Central Avenue bus, take it to the terminal, and head farther north on foot until I reach her house. It was kind of a pain in the ass, but at the time, it was so worth it. Nancy was a few years younger than me. Never had a boyfriend. Very naive in the ways of the world. I knew this going in, so I tried to be very understanding. Never mind the fact I was still trying to figure out this opposite-sex thing. I was no Mr. Smooth either. The more time we spent together, the closer we became. The uncomfortable fumbling began once again. I'd got the French-kiss thing down pretty good. I tried desperately to go further. Every move I made got shot down, except one. Nancy had no objection to me grabbing her ass. Either on the outside of her pants or underneath her pants. We made out and played grab ass for hours. I was fine with that.

*****

On occasion, I'd toss in another move, and I'd get shot down. You can't blame a guy for trying. Seeing Nancy was still very young, she had a very early curfew. In response to that, I tried and kept our dates as close to her house as possible. Her parents didn't mind if I hung out with her at their house after curfew. This gave me a great idea. How would you like me to bring over some booze, watch a little TV downstairs, and play a little grab ass? Nancy was game. I asked her what she would like me to grab (steal), and she said Sangria. I had no idea what that was, but by damn, I'd get it. Earlier in the week, I grabbed two bottles of Yago Sangria and sneaked them into my room. Friday night, I hopped on the Central Avenue bus on my way to Nancy's house. Upon my arrival, I exchanged pleasantries with her mother (her father hated me from the get-go, so he never spoke a word to me), and we headed off to the basement for some TV time. Right. We turned the TV on, turned the lights off, and cracked open a bottle. We drank directly from the bottle because Mr. Smooth had forgotten to bring glasses. We polished off the first bottle rather quickly. I'd caught a pretty good buzz. Nancy, from what I could tell, was flying (I'm not sure she has ever drunk any booze in her short lifetime). We cracked open the second bottle, and each took a swig. We placed the bottle to the side and lay down on the carpeted floor. We started making out, and within five minutes, I had my hand down the inside of her very, very tight jeans. The longer we made out, the lower my hand went.

Suddenly, the overhead lights flashed on. "Nancy!" It was her mother! Holy shit! Nancy shot up, forgetting my hand was down her pants. It almost broke off. I scrambled to my knees while trying to extricate my hand from her backside. I finally freed myself and stood up. Nancy's mother was screaming at her, and they were both crying. As I scanned the room, I saw the empty wine bottle on one side, the other tipped over, and the dark purple wine was soaking into the tan carpet. I had no idea what the fuck to do. I picked up the two bottles, placed them back into the bag, and whispered, "Maybe I should go." Neither Nancy nor her mother looked my way or said a word to me. They kept screaming at each other in Polish (so I had no idea what the hell they were saying) as I made my exit. Well, that was interesting. I headed back south.

The night was still young. I wondered what Ricky was up to. Without hesitation (or another thought about the mess I just made), I headed his way. As luck would have it, he was home. We grabbed some booze from his room and headed out. I told him about my night, and we laughed and laughed. Does it get any better than this? Of course, Nancy was grounded for the next two weeks. No problem. I'd find something else to do in her absence. I had quite a few drinking buddies (girls and boys) to choose from! I didn't skip a beat.

*****

Life at Johnson settled into a familiar pattern once again. I still loved my job and worked very hard at it. I take pride in what I do. I wanted to be the best stock boy in the world. That said, when the work was done, I didn't mind messing around a bit. A good evening would start like this. A few deliveries out the back door and ten to fifteen bucks into my pocket. I headed for the refrigerated section of the store. We not only carried cold beer and wine; we had a fairly large food section. Lunch meat, milk, ice cream, etc. I'd steal a loaf of bread from the other side of the store and bring it with me through the back door of the refrigerated box. I would grab a package of lunch meat, tear it open, put the entire content between two pieces of bread, and chow down. I'd then grab a half gallon of chocolate milk and wash the one-pound sandwich down. Now that was eating good in the neighborhood. Oh yeah, dessert. I would pop the lid off one of the whip cream cylinders, hold it upright, and shoot it directly into my mouth. Three or four squirts later, I would put the cap back on and put it back on the shelf. I couldn't begin to tell you how much joy I would get seeing some old lady purchasing one of my tainted whip cream cylinders. Not too fucked up, eh? Once mealtime was over, I would head to the southwest corner of the store. Located in that corner was a very large safe where we kept all the large bills and rolled coins. I would grab a *Penthouse Forum* from the liquor department, climb up onto the safe, and sit cross-legged while I read the magazine, cover to cover, waiting for my shift to end so I could head home. Booze, food, money, and porn. Again, it doesn't get any better than that!

*****

As life went on, I settled into a pattern that would become a weekly routine for the rest of my time in high school. I would work my ass off during the week. No time for any fun and games between school, work, and homework. Friday, and especially Saturday night, was a whole different ball game. When the store would close at 9:00 p.m., there was always part of my crew waiting for me. Ricky, Laura, Kathy, etc. Sometimes it would be only one. Other times, it would be all. It didn't really matter. We were going to do what we do best—stay out late, get as drunk as we could, and have a great time shooting the shit. We would do this on both Friday and Saturday nights. Every night, we would drink something different—beer, Boone's Farm (that shit was like Kool-Aid), Mad Dog 20/20, vodka and orange soda (from the local Burger King), Canadian Club, etc. We didn't give a shit as long as we got wasted. These were such therapeutic sessions for me. It gave me a chance to unwind and talk about my bullshit life. I was a very, very angry young man at this point in my life, and I desperately needed this outlet. Even with this outlet, I still had a ton of pent-up frustration. Guess who I took that out on? My parents, of course. They tried so hard to keep me in line, but I was already gone. I'd come home drunk every weekend, and they would ground me.

"Fuck you, you're grounded!" would be my standard response. My mom would slap me, and I would just laugh, saying, "That didn't hurt! Try it again! You can do better than that!" Of course, it hurt, but I never let on that it did. She'd hit me again, and I would laugh. After about five minutes of this game, I would tire and head off to bed, looking to repeat this process all over again tomorrow night. I know I was being a dick. In my mind, when they pulled the carpet out from under me earlier in the year, I told myself, *I'm on my own. Nobody is going to tell me what to do!* Let me share with you a few more stories about this time in my life. Just how crazy things were getting.

*****

Back in January 1979, my friend Kathy had decided to throw a party one Saturday night. Just a few friends. Adult supervised, so things didn't get out of control. Pop, chips, pizza, cookies. Pretty lame shit, but we decided to go because it was something different. Or not. Prior to heading into the party, Larry, Laura, and I grabbed three RC colas from my fridge. We headed up to my bedroom to grab whatever booze was most convenient in my stash. It looked like we'd be drinking tequila tonight. We each poured out about three quarters of our cans and replaced the soda with tequila. We headed on out to Kathy's house (about two blocks away, straight east). We headed on up where the party was in full swing. We listened to music, talked about God knows what, and sipped our pop. Well, some of us sipped. Others (me) too stupid to stretch things out a bit proceeded to guzzle the pop-and-booze mixture. I was done in less than ten minutes. Not much longer after that, I was drunk out of my mind. I got loud. I got obnoxious. The few in the in thought it was funny as hell. Those who weren't in the in thought I was some kind of nut. Believe me, I get it.

After about thirty minutes of ranting and raving, for some reason, I decided to go for a walk. Mind you, the temperature was single digits, and there was a good six to eight inches of snow on the ground. I stumbled out of my chair, barely able to stand. I headed for the front door, not a word spoken to anyone. Kathy lived in a two-flat on the second floor. It took me a good five to ten minutes to make my way down the steps and out the front door. While I stood on the sidewalk, I had a vague idea which way to go and where I lived. I started heading west on Roscoe Street. After what seemed like *forever* (I had no sense of time or direction at this time), I made it to the street I lived on (I think?). I came up with a great idea. Instead of heading straight through the front door to play my weekly games with my mother, I was going to make my way through the alley, up the back steps of the house, and quietly head up to my bedroom, where I could hit the sack. After another thirty minutes or so passing, I found the gate to my backyard. Mind you, it was taking me a good hour to walk two blocks and find my home. I fumbled with the latch, and in my drunken state, I could not figure out for the life of me how to get it open. I got frustrated. I got angry. Most importantly, I got tired. I decided I was going to take a break. I'd just sit down on this snowbank and rest my eyes for a minute.

The next thing I know, I felt somebody shaking me and calling out my name. "Bob! Bob! Wake up!" My eyes came into focus. It was my mother. She was standing over me in the alley, desperately trying to wake me up.

"Where am I?" As the words left my mouth, my breath hit my mom in the face and ricocheted back into mine. It smelled like a fucking gin mill. Her eyes opened like a raging bull. She was pissed and attempted to pull me out of the snowbank. As I stumbled forward, I realized I left the party without my hat, gloves, or coat! I was dressed in sweatpants and a T-shirt. Holy shit! I could have died. Thank God my mom went out to pitch the garbage and saw my silhouette in the snow or God knows how this story would end. We made our way into the house. We played our game. Instead of being grateful, I said "Fuck you" and headed off to bed. While I was passed out, my mother called down to Kathy's house and spoke to her mom. She read her the riot act for serving booze to minors. Of course, she had no idea what my mom was talking about. The party was shut down. Kathy got in big trouble. It was not her fault; it was mine. Such was life.

*****

The following week, Tony, Ricky, and I decided to hit the local pizza joint. Poretta's served the best deep-dish pizza around. As always, our eyes were bigger than our stomach. We knocked off about half the pizza before we called it quits. Of course, throughout the meal, we were smoking and joking, spilling pop, dropping pizza on the floor, whatever. The manager finally came over to the table to read us the riot act.

"Shut up or get the hell out?"

Are you talking to me? My head started spinning because I was so pissed off. We decided it was dine-and-dash time. We grabbed the leftover pizza and headed for the exit. We were out. As we loaded into Tony's car, we were laughing our asses off (at least Ricky and I were, Tony knew we just broke the law, and he was a bit nervous). Just then, a great idea popped into my head. We were not going to eat this pizza. We needed to save it, put it to good use. Just like the Society for the Prevention of Cruelty to Doughnuts, we needed to do something "creative." We developed a plan on the spot. Tony pulled his car up to the back entrance of the restaurant. There was a door there for pickup orders. Ricky and I grabbed a big slice in each hand and headed inside. We rang the pickup bell. A few seconds later, a lady and a man came around the corner in front of the counter. We let it fly! Again, *bang, splat, crack!* We had several direct hits to the signage as well as to our innocent victims. Now getting hit with a doughnut was one thing. Getting hit with a full piece of cheese- and sausage-stuffed pizza was a whole other thing. These people were knocked sideways. The signage was cracked. We headed for the exits.

For some reason, Tony put the car into reverse. We blasted backward, directly into a snow bank. Tony panicked. He was gunning the engine while throwing the gear shifter into drive, reverse, drive, reverse. Suddenly, the back door of the restaurant shot open. It was the manager, with three other big burly guys, heading straight for us. Thank God Tony was able to free the car. We blasted backward as we fishtailed into the street. Tony slammed it into drive, and we were off like a shot. As Tony was sweating bullets, Ricky and I were laughing our asses off. Another successful adventure! I guess we wouldn't be eating at Poretta's any time in the near future. Wait, the night was not over just yet. We saved the best for last.

*****

This story takes us back to Boy Scouts. Don't ask me how or why, but both Ricky and I made it all the way through Cub Scouts, Webelos, and eventually, "walked the bridge" to enter Boy Scouts. When making this journey, the Boy Scouts would give you this beautiful arrow. It's bright yellow, with beautiful markings, brown-and-white feather at one end, with a razor-sharp tip at the other. These arrows were supposed to symbolize your journey from Cub Scouts to Boy Scouts. For me, it had the opposite symbolism. It symbolized the nightmare I lived during this period of my life. Now, for whatever reason, we both had our arrows in the car. After our latest escapade, we still had a ton of energy and anger running through our veins. We decided to head back to Ricky's house and have some fun with these arrows. Ricky and his father were big hunters. This gave him access to a hunting bow. He'd shot it before and knew how to use it.

"What a perfect way to signal the end of Scouts!"

He headed into the house and emerged with a bow. We headed to the alley. We decided we were going to shoot these arrows all over the neighborhood. He went first. He pulled back and let loose with a perfect shot into a neighbor's garage door. I was next. He showed me what to do, but I struggled. My first shot sailed into a neighbor's yard. We retrieved my arrow and continued on. Three, four, five shots. I was getting better. On my sixth shot, I buried that arrow into one of the wooden telephone poles. As the tip buried itself into the wood, the shaft of the arrow splintered into several sections and dropped to the ground.

"Success!"

The arrow was completely destroyed. I left the remaining tip in the pole as a symbol of my hatred for the Scouts. Ricky decided he was going to be like Robin Hood. He was going to shoot his arrow through the remaining piece of my arrow. After several missed attempts, he was finally successful.

"That's one hell of a shot!"

The tip of his arrow was now buried into the back of mine, his shaft in the same condition as mine. We smiled from ear to ear. That was one hell of a way to end a crazy evening.

*****

As the weather warmed up, we started spending more time exploring the streets of Chicago. One Friday night, I decided to walk up to Ricky's place of employment. It was still cool outside, but it was a perfect night for a nice long walk. I got off work at 9:00 p.m., headed home to grab what booze I had, and headed west to Harlem and Irving. It was a good two- to three-mile trek, so I had to get going pretty quick. Ricky got off later, so it should time out perfectly. For the evening, I chose a six-pack of Michelob and a half gallon of Crown Royal (our favorite at the time, you can tell based on the fact the bottle is already three-quarters empty). I had no idea what time I arrived. It didn't matter because we were in no hurry to get home. We had all night to walk, drink, and bullshit. We headed south down Harlem Avenue, then turned east down Irving Park road. Both were major thoroughfares in the city (four-lane roads, two lanes in each direction). Don't ask us why we were not walking down the side streets. I guess we were feeling ballsy that particular night. Ricky carried the six-pack container in his left hand and an open beer in his right. I carried the half gallon of Crown Royal in my left hand and a half-drunken beer in my right. The evening was just getting started. We had drunk so very little to this point neither of us had a buzz yet. A few minutes passed, and a Chicago patrol car passed us on the right. We were on the north side of the street. They were on the south side heading east. As they passed, Ricky and I raised our beers in salute of Chicago's finest. Not the brightest bulbs on the tree, eh? Of course, the police officers saw us and made an immediate U-turn, pulling right up next to us on the sidewalk.

"Do you think that was funny, you dumbasses? What would compel you to toast a police officer?"

Who the hell knew what we were thinking? They confiscated the booze and threw it in the trunk. They threw us both into the back of their squad car.

"Names and addresses, stupid fucks."

In a whisper, we provided them with the information they requested. As we started driving, it became quite apparent we were not going to the police station (based on the direction we were going). It appeared they were taking us home. First stop, my house. One of the officers grabbed the alcohol out of the trunk, and the four of us headed up the front stairs. They rang the bell, and my mom answered the door. They introduced themselves and asked to come in, Ricky and I following behind. They told their story to my parents while they placed the whiskey and six-pack on the living room coffee table. My parents acted shock. They acted like I'd never been in contact with booze in my life. It was that night I got another nickname connected to me that we (Ricky and I primarily) laugh about to this day.

"What do you have to say for yourself *Mr. Bleary Eyes*?"

My only defense was, "We only had one beer. We just started drinking."

Of course, my mom told me to stop lying on top of everything else. "We know what you did!" My parents were under the impression that on top of the one beer each that we had drunk, we also polished off a half gallon off hard stuff. Are you kidding me? We'd be dead. There was no arguing with them. I took my lumps, and the police handed me over to my parents. Once again, I avoided worst-case scenario. I lived a charmed life. Of course, I was grounded for a year, and I was never to see Ricky again. Seriously? I saw him next Friday, like so many Fridays to come. As for Ricky, it was an even better ending for him. The cops went to his house, and his parents weren't home. They dropped him off and told him to speak with his parents upon their return. He was a good kid. He did tell them, and they gave him a speech about right and wrong. What could have been a real mess turned out to be a slap on the wrist. As I said, I hooked up with Ricky the following Friday. All the BS about being grounded and not hanging with my best friend, stick it up your ass!

I continued to do whatever I wanted. The icing on the cake? I stole back the beer and booze from my parents, and we made a huge dent in it that evening. Youth gone wild, my friends.

*****

As you have read throughout this book, the creativity and imagination we used during this time period was second to none. We never did the simple, standard stuff. We always strived to be creative in whatever we did. Case in point. It was the spring of 1979. Ricky and I were on one of our walks once again. We might have had a few cocktails before heading out. We took a walk north, heading to one of our favorite haunts, Portage Park. The park was huge and had many, many places to hang out and be unseen. We talked for hours, never running out of things to say to each other. It was the middle of the night, and we decided to keep moving. We found ourselves walking through a back alley just north of the park. Off in the darkness, we saw the silhouette of a mattress laying up against the side of a garage. As we got a closer look, we saw it was totally roached out. Stinky, smelly, dirty, stains everywhere. Our brains kicked into overdrive.

"What can we do with this?"

The light bulb went on once again. A very good friend of ours, Mark, lived about three to four blocks from there. Wouldn't it be outstanding if we could somehow get this mattress to his house? We didn't know at the time what the hell we'd do with it when we got it there. We'd figure that out later. We each grabbed an end of the mattress and headed off toward Mark's house. Down side streets. Across busy intersections. Down alleys. Basically, in full view of everyone's paths that we crossed. Nobody stopped us. Nobody said a word. It was like two high school boys and a king-size mattress were invisible. We finally arrived at Mark's house. After a bit of back-and-forth, we decided what we were going to do. We leaned the mattress up against the front door, rang the bell three to four times, and hauled ass down the street. We were laughing uncontrollably as we made our way back to Portage Park. It was one thing to do a little ding-dong ditch. Kids did it all the time. It was a whole other thing to be awakened at 12:30 a.m. to a filthy mattress lying on your front porch. We conjured up the look on their faces and laughed until we cried. I could not imagine what went through their minds at the split second they opened that door. Not to mention, you now have to move that greasy mattress, in your robe and slippers, in the middle of the night, from your porch to your back alley. How grand!

The night, however, was not over. Our creative juices were still flowing. After all this excitement, Ricky had to take a shit. We were too far from home, and there was nothing open at this time. He had to improvise. Now you can do what 99.9 percent of the rest of the world would do. Find a dark corner and do your business. Boring. As we walked through the park, we took note of all the picnic benches that had been laid out. Here was an idea. Let's take those benches and make a pyramid. Once complete, Ricky could climb that pyramid and do his thing on the top of the benches. Ricky climbed up like a little monkey, dropped his draws, laid a big old turd, wiped his ass, and climbed down. As we walked home, we were once again laughing so hard tears were running down our faces. We thought ahead to the following day, when the park workers would go to undo our pyramid and find the prize that we left. It was classic. To this day, I still tear up thinking about it. Definitely an A for creativity. That was one hell of a night!

*****

Speaking of nights, let's fast-forward a few more weeks. Once again, I met Ricky at his place of employment. The sole purpose of my visit was to walk him home and polish off a pint of Canadian Club in the process (one of our favorite pastimes was to walk for miles and catch a buzz). It was still cold out, and there was a bit of snow on the ground. In Chicago, it was common practice to put any kind of junk in the street to save the shoveled space in the front of your home—chairs, tables, couches, whatever was most convenient and large enough to cover your space. As we were walking, we were making note of all the crap we saw. We came across a house about a mile from Ricky's work. In the front of that house was a big old sawhorse. For whatever reason, we took exception to this particular item. We both knocked back a big old shot of CC and prepared to destroy that sawhorse in the middle of the street (again, don't ask me why). We laughed and yelled as we smashed it down repeatedly until it was nothing but a pile of kindling in the middle of the street. We were very proud of our accomplishments. We downed another swig and headed for home. A few blocks up, we saw a big old white van, doing about seventy miles per hour, bright lights on, heading our way. It screeched to a stop about a hundred yards away from where Ricky and I were walking in the street.

A big old burley guy jumped out, two-by-four in his hand, screaming, "I'm going to kill you, little sons of bitches!"

We put two and two together. He must be the owner of the sawhorse. We took off running. This guy jumped back into his van, and he was hot on our heels. We were scared shitless. We made our way to St. Joseph's Cemetery at Oak Park and Addison Avenue and scaled the fence. This guy couldn't follow us in because the gates were locked and he was too big to jump the fence. We watched from the darkness as he circled the lot. We lay low for about an hour, hoping the coast was clear, then made our way to the east side of the cemetery. There was no sign of him. We scaled the fence and ran the entire way home. We sat down on a bench in Chopin Park, winded as all hell, to review the evening's events and to polish off the balance of our pint. Of course, as we drank more, we went from being frightened to being emboldened.

"What an asshole! All we did was break a sawhorse! What's the big deal! We'll show that guy who's boss!"

We spent the rest of the night planning our revenge. The following weekend, we enlisted Tony to drive us back to the guy's house. We instructed him to park halfway down the alley and to wait for us, engine running. We each had a handful of fireworks and a lighter. We sneaked around the corner, lit each of the firecrackers (M-80s, if my memory serves me correctly), and lobbed them one by one into the gutters on the top of his house. *Bam! Bam! Bam!* The explosions were loud as hell. The damage was significant. Pieces of the gutters and roofing material were shooting everywhere. We hauled ass down the alley, jumped into Tony's car, and squealed off into the night. Again, the adrenaline was flowing. We were as high as a kite.

"That was awesome! We sure showed him!"

We headed over to Central Gyros to grab a sandwich and a pitcher of beer to celebrate our success. A week later, we found ourselves out on a Friday night with not much to do. We were once again cruising around in Tony's car. A great idea popped into my head.

"Why don't we pay our friend another visit?"

Tony vetoed that idea immediately. Ricky and I thought it was a great idea and rode his ass for the next thirty minutes until he reluctantly agreed. This time, we decided to inflict some damage to his van. We pulled a tire iron from the truck of the car. We cruised the back alleys until we found a piece of pipe. Again, Tony parked halfway up the back alley. Ricky and I armed ourselves and headed for the front of the house. There it sat. This beautiful white van with windows bumper to bumper. We went to town. I started at the front windshield as Ricky started on the right side. We worked our way, front to back, finishing off with the very large back window. When we were finished, every window of the van was knocked out. We made our way back to the car and took off. The deed was done. I guess we really showed him. Not once did we stop and think that the punishment did not fit the crime. We broke a sawhorse and got chased around (rightfully so) for a bit. Does that give us the right to inflict thousands of dollars of damage to this poor guy's home and vehicle? Hell yes, it does! Youth gone wild!

*****

It was now the summer of 1979. I'd made it through my junior year of high school. Not only have I survived high school to date, I've actually thrived. I was not sure how, but my grades to this point had been solid (B+ average). Between going to school six hours a day, working forty to fifty hours a week and drinking/gallivanting around with the balance of my free time, I was still able to keep it all together. God, it was good to be young and energetic! There was one evening in the summer of 1979 that I will never forget. It really is a summation of just how creative and crazy we were back then. Ricky (yes, Ricky once again) and I were at Chopin Park just hanging out. In the playground was a group of older kids fucking around. The problem we had was, they were getting a bit destructive—tying up the swings, lighting off fireworks and throwing them in the sandbox. Now normally this would not bother us, seeing it was some of the same stuff we would generally be doing. The problem was, there were still younger kids in the park as this was going on. They looked scared. Their parents were uneasy.

"What a bunch of dicks!"

Once again, that nasty old light bulb went on. We headed back to Ricky's house and picked up a shit ton of bottle rockets he had tucked away in his bedroom. We headed back to the park. By now, all the little kids have left the park, leaving the older kids to their mayhem and destruction. We hatched a plan. There was a four-foot-high chain-link fence that surrounded the park. We took a half-dozen bottle rockets and stuck the shafts in the top links. They were pointed directly at the wild Indians. We lit them off simultaneously (three each) and watched them whizz by the older kids. They were stunned. They were shocked. For a few seconds, we both stopped and stared at each other. Once it came into focus on what just happened, they started screaming out and started running our way. We took off immediately, heading east toward the St. Ladislaus parking lot. We ran around the back side of the school. What the hell were we going to do? The light bulb went on once again. We lined up God knows how many bottle rockets on the top of the asphalt. We decided that, as our pursuers turned the corner, we were going to light the bottle rockets off in their direction.

"Here they come!"

We went right down the line. One, two, three, four… They went ripping off in all directions. The kids heard/saw them and scattered, ducking for cover. It was like a scene out of a war movie. We lit off a few more and doubled back toward the park.

"Wait a minute, I've got a question. What the hell are we running for?"

There was nobody on our tail. In fact, there was nobody in sight. It was eerily quiet. We took a seat on a bench in the northwest corner of the park. We were once again smiling from ear to ear.

"We really showed those guys!"

We took back our park and could not be happier. This particular night we each had a half pint of Seagram's Seven. We pulled the bottles out of our back pockets, clinked them together in a toast, took a big old swig, and celebrated our success. What could we do to top that? We decided to head west and do some exploring. It was a very hot night, and we were looking for some way to cool ourselves off. Just west of Central Avenue, we decided to ditch our shoes and shirts in some bushes and do a bit of pool hopping. We headed down the alley and scoped out the backyards. We found our first pool and slinked in. The yard was dark; the water was cool. How refreshing. We slithered back out and continued our journey. We were fortunate enough to find several other pools within close proximity and continued our escapades. As we sneaked into our next pool, we could not help but see that the yard was full of plastic yard animals—geese, deer, raccoons. How cool would it be to put those animals into the swimming pool with us? In they came, one by one. It was not enough for us to have these animals bobbing around in the pool. We decided to line them up in the water and for us to start swimming around the edge of the pool, creating a circular current. The faster we swam, the faster the animals made their way around the pool. Of course, by now, we had one hell of a buzz going on, and we were laughing our asses off, louder and louder. All of a sudden, a light turned on at the back porch of the house.

"What the hell is going on out there? Who the hell is out there?"

Ricky and I bolted from the pool and headed for the back gate. We blasted our way out and headed east down the alley. As I looked back over my shoulder, all I could see was the yard animals zipping around the outer edge of the pool, one right behind the other. I could not help but smile and begin laughing uncontrollably. I thought to myself, *What in the hell must be going through the homeowner's mind? To come outside and see a half-dozen plastic yard animals swimming in your pool?* What an excellent mental picture! Harmless fun. Creative as hell. One hell of a way to spend a hot summer's night in the city!

*****

1979–1980

It was now the fall of 1979. I was heading into my senior year at St. Patrick's High School. At this point in my life, I had no clue what the hell I was going to do after this year. I had gone through the motions of taking my ACTs (actually scored pretty well) and sent off college applications to every local school I could think of. I didn't have any idea on where I wanted to go or what I wanted to study. I was so focused on work (making money) and hanging out with my friends (partying) I couldn't give two shits about my future. By this point, I had made so much money (both through my legit paycheck and my illegal activities) that I had my eyes set on buying a car. My parents had taken me to get my license but, again, would *never* allow me to take the car. Based on my behavior, could you blame them? Of course, at that age, it really pissed me off, but there was not a whole hell of a lot I could do. I searched the ads in the paper. I walked the used car lots. I finally found a car that I immediately fell in love with. It was a 1972 Charger, bright red with a black vinyl top and black leather interior. It was totally tricked out. It was the most beautiful thing I had ever seen. It was parked on the Shell gas station parking lot at Belmont and Long Avenue. I went to the lot every day to take a good long look at it. The price was a bit high, but I had enough money saved (in my *own* savings account) to buy this baby!

I went home one evening and told my parents I had found a car I planned on buying. I shared every detail I could about my baby. They told me I was too young and immature to own my own car. I went nuts! I was going to school full-time and working full-time (because of you!). How much more mature and responsible could I be? I started off by debating and negotiating. That went nowhere fast. I switched to screaming, yelling, and swearing.

"Fuck you! I'm buying this car, and there's not a damn thing you can do about it!"

Then the bomb dropped. My parents informed me that I was not old enough to buy a car on my own, that I needed them to cosign, and that based on my behavior and language, it was never going to happen in a million years! Once again, I was fucked over. I couldn't use their car. I couldn't buy my own. You just couldn't win. My relationship with my parents took another step backward. As a senior, I was stuck taking the bus or hoofing it. Welcome to my world.

*****

In January of 1980, all St. Pat seniors had to attend an off-site religious retreat. Every week, forty to fifty boys were packed into a school bus and transported to the center located in Plano, Illinois. There we would learn about love, trust, God, etc. Of course, nothing we gave a shit about back then. January 14 came around, and it was my turn to attend. Thank God I got to go with several of my best friends at the time—Ricky, Mark, Joey, etc. Upon arrival at the facility, we were given a brief facility tour then taken to our assigned rooms. Our rooms were in a two-story building, just north of the main building, connected by a long hallway. It looked and was set up exactly like Holiday Inn (hotel). The rooms consisted of a single bed in one corner, a table, chair-and-lamp combination in the other, and a small sofa/love seat with a coffee table in the center. There was a shared shower/washroom located in the center of each floor. To our utter shock and amazement, we found out we were in this section of the building all by ourselves (all the counselors will be sleeping in another part of the facility). Fifty high school boys, with no adult supervision, free to do whatever they want during break times and in the evening. Holy shit! I was not sure whose idea this was, but I knew immediately this was going to be good. We unpacked our suitcases and made our way to the main living area. It was a huge building with hardwood floors, overstuffed couches, and a huge brick fireplace. Quite cozy.

Our first exercise was going to be meditation. We were told how to clear our minds and to focus on our "happy place." The lights were dimmed as some soft, peaceful music was pumped in over the strategically placed speakers. Not even thirty seconds in, the first fart was heard, followed by a few giggles. Not even ten seconds later, the second. Before you know it, everyone was pushing out farts, each one louder and longer than the last. The place went crazy with farts and laughter. The lights came back on, and we were all reprimanded for our behavior.

Next, we were going to see a film on some bullshit activity. I cannot remember the subject matter, but it was boring as hell. The lights went down once again, and the film started up. Within minutes, you would hear the low rumble of a snore. Then another and another… We were dropping like flies. I passed out. A few minutes later, I was awoken from my slumber by one of the counselors pulling me across the hardwood floor by my legs. I was not the only one. There goes Ricky, followed by Joey. Half the class was being dragged out of the room. We were now told to sit in silence in the corner and to not move. No speaking. Of course, we laughed and fucked around. Miraculously, we made it to lunchtime. We had thirty minutes to eat, followed by thirty minutes of quiet time in our rooms. Quiet time in our rooms? Are you kidding me? Ricky and I sat at a table and laid out our plans for "quiet time." We wolfed down our food and headed back to the hotel.

Our buddy Mark's room was the next room over from Ricky's. We blasted into his room and just went crazy. We turned over his bed. We threw his clothes all over the room. We took big wads of toilet paper, soaked them down, and stuck them to the walls, the ceiling, the windows. We took his toothpaste out and squeezed it all over his clean clothes. The room was an absolute disaster! We went screaming out into the hallway and headed back to the main room. We were laughing uncontrollably, tears in our eyes. Ten minutes later, Mark wandered back into the hall. As we were shedding tears of joy, Mark was shedding tears of anguish and anger. He knew who was responsible for this disaster and made it very clear he was going to retaliate in some form or fashion. Before you know it, we were all laughing our asses off at what just happened. More importantly, what lay in store?

Fast-forward a bit. It was now evening time, and we were dismissed back to our rooms for the evening. As expected, it was a total free-for-all in the hotel. Kids were running up and down the hall, screaming like wild Indians, throwing shit at one another, blasting in and out of doors. Ricky and I were hunkered down in his room, located right next door to Joey's room. Mark was in there with him. We knew they were plotting some kind of revenge for our early activities. We pounded on the wall. They pounded back. We shouted curse words at one another, each time getting louder and louder (followed by laughter). Then things went silent. What the hell was going on? All of a sudden, something came flying out of the sky and landed on the floor. We picked it up. It was a piece of soap.

"What the hell? Where did that come from?"

As we were scanning the room, another piece came flying in. It was coming from the corner of the ceiling and the wall. We pushed the table next to the wall and climbed up. As we reached the area from where the soap came from, we realized the ceiling was louvered. There were basically holes you could look through to see the light coming from the other room. Ingenious! I didn't know how these guys discovered this, but it was outstanding. For the next hour, we found things to fire back at one another—soap, toothbrushes, pens, etc. We tried to one up one another. The heavier and longer, the better. That damn light bulb came on once again! I headed to the closet. In the closet were your standard-issue hangers for the time. They were made of thin metal rod with a paper sleeve covering the center of the hanger. Ricky and I grabbed a handful and headed back to the table. We took the first one and flattened it down as much as we could. It was far enough down that it would fit through the hole in the wall.

This was where most people would stop. Not Ricky and me. How could we make this even better? I ran to my suitcase and pulled out a Bic lighter. As Ricky held the smashed hanger, I lit the paper sleeve on fire. As soon as it was burning, we shot it through the wall. *Bam!* It flew through and appeared to hit a lamp, which, of course, fell to the floor, breaking into a million pieces. There was absolute silence on the other side. Then we heard "Holy shit" followed by a bunch of shuffling around.

"Top that one off, you bastards!"

Ricky and I were on the floor in the fetal position, laughing so hard our bellies were aching. The door opened, and in walked Mark and Joey, looking like they just saw a ghost. We couldn't stop laughing. Their light was broken, and their carpet was singed. They were here to call a truce. Ricky's room was covered in debris as the four of us recounted the evening's events and laughed our asses off. After another hour or so, we decided to call it a night. I was exhausted and needed to get some shut-eye. Even with all the noise in the hallway, it was not long until I passed out. All of a sudden, I heard a noise coming from the entryway of my bedroom. I lifted my head up from my pillow as the door to my room swung violently open. I could make out the shadow of an object heading straight toward me. It ricocheted off the left side of my head and came crashing to a halt against the wall just behind me. It was wet. It smelled terrible. As I switched on the light, I could see it was an old, filthy, disgusting mop! They must have found it in the bathroom and figured it would make a great weapon (they were right!). As my eyes came further into focus, I could hear my attackers running down the hallway, laughing their asses off. Well played, boys!

After zero hours of sleep, we got into our second day. More of the same bullshit. Will this ever end? At lunchtime, Ricky and I decided to go for a walk and explore the campus a bit more. No hat, coat, or gloves. We headed out in our blue jeans and flannel shirts. Again, where was the supervision? We could have died from exposure, and they wouldn't have found us until the springtime. We wrapped up the afternoon sessions and headed back to our rooms to pack up. This was the *first* time any of the counselors or brothers came to check on us to make sure everything was cool. They were absolutely shocked at what they found and saw. The place was filthy. Destruction everywhere. The hotel was an absolute disaster. At first, they said nothing. We got on the bus to head home. As we were pulling out of the driveway, the head brother let us have it. He was pissed beyond belief. After twenty to thirty minutes of reading us the riot act, he went on to inform us that St. Patrick High School would never be allowed back to that facility ever again.

"I hope you are happy that you have ruined this for all the future classes to come!"

Cool! I just wished someone had done that for us so we could have skipped all the bullshit. Youth gone wild, my friend.

*****

Speaking of brothers, I would be remiss without a mention of Brother John. I managed to skip taking chemistry (I hated it) until my senior year. It was mandatory that you complete this course if you want to graduate. Brother John would be my instructor for this class. Upon my arrival, it was quite apparent that another guy and I were the only two seniors in this class. All the rest were freshman or sophomores. We felt completely out of place. How do we respond? We immediately became the class clowns. When attendance was taken, we would yell into our hands, "Bullshit!" As Brother John was trying to teach, we were trying to distract him anyway we could—dropping books, throwing pencils, making puking sounds. Anything we could think of. Brother spent half his class trying to determine who was being disruptive. Of course, there was no freshman or sophomore in this world who was going to squeal on a senior. The chaos continued on a daily basis.

One day, I got to class a few minutes early. A film projector was set up in the back of the class. I got this great idea. My job at Johnson called for me to carry and use a box cutter throughout the day. As a result, I had one in my back pocket at all times. I shot to the back of the room, loosened the film on the reel, sliced through it with my box cutter, tightened it back up the best I could, and returned to my seat before the rest of the class arrived. The room filled up. Brother John started up the projector. About five minutes in, the film came to a halt. The back spindle kept spinning; film was rapidly piling up on the floor. The front spindle had stopped completely. The film on that front section began to smoke and catch on fire. Brother John was in panic mode. He grabbed a fire extinguisher and put the fire out. He then pulled the plug on the equipment. After catching his breath, he assessed the damage. It was a total loss—the projector, the film. He called downstairs to both the principal as well as the AV department. They both arrived almost instantaneously. As Bother John and the principal discussed the situation, the AV guy inspected the projector.

"It appears someone has tampered with the film. There is too clean a cut for this to be an accident or equipment failure."

The class went dead silent, with the exception of me, who was now purple in the face trying to hold back my laughter.

"Sorensen, did you have anything to do with this?"

Of course, I lied and said, "Oh no, I would never do anything like that." They could hear the sarcasm in my voice. They asked several more times, and several more times I lied. They finally told me to report to the dean's office immediately. Upon arrival, I told him what happened. My punishment? "You are to report to detention first thing in the morning and will remain there for the next two weeks." I chuckled to myself as I exited his office. Seeing I had been in detention since my freshman year (I still refuse to keep my hair at the required length), this punishment was nothing to me. I learned absolutely nothing from this experience other than to think I was untouchable. The escapades continued. One day, Brother left the room, and my partner in crime and I threw every piece of paper we could find out the third-story window into the courtyard below. Detention. Another day, I arrived early once again and loosened the bolts on one of the desks adjacent to mine. When the poor freshman hit the seat, he immediately tumbled to the floor in a heap of wood and metal. Detention. This went on for several months. As for my grade, you can just imagine. I'd spent more time fucking around than focusing on my studies. I had flunked every quiz, every test. I had completed very little of my homework.

It was now early December, and it was time for parent-teacher conferences. They sent a note home with me that I immediately threw into the trash. They sent another one, then another. All of them met with the same fate. Eventually, they called home and spoke to my mother. Of course, she had no idea what they were talking about. She insisted she and my dad would be there tomorrow. When I got home, my mom went nuts on me.

"You're flunking chemistry, and we know nothing about it? You've been throwing notes meant for us in the garbage?"

I stopped her in her tracks. "What the fuck is it to you? I'm paying for my own education, so you have no say in what I do! This is my business, mine alone!"

Of course, that didn't fly. The next day, we went to see Brother John. He went into great detail about not only my grades but also my constant disruptions in his class. He then went on to say that deep down I was a good kid who would certainly do well if I applied myself. No shit, Sherlock! My parents shook his hand and took their exit. Brother pulled me aside and said we'd both try harder to get through the second half of the year and get me on my way to college. Yeah right! After my return from Christmas break, I picked up where I left off. More of the same shit. I hadn't learned a damn thing. Remember, I was untouchable.

I added a new activity to my repertoire. When a quiz was handed out and I didn't know the answers, I wouldn't even attempt to guess. On the line where the answer was supposed to be provided, I put the name of my favorite heavy metal groups.

Hydrogen and oxygen combine to make = Black Sabbath.

The process of turning carbon dioxide into oxygen is called = Iron Maiden.

You get the drift. Brother John continued to meet with me weekly. He was in constant contact with my parents. As of mid-February, I was hovering around the 40 percentile in this class. I needed a 70 percent to pass. I had thrown in the towel. I didn't give a shit at this point in time. It was now May, and we were taking our final exams. I actually buckled down and studied my ass off in preparation for each of my classes, including chemistry. I made it through the week, feeling pretty good about how I did. I realized that regardless of how I did on my finals, I was, in all likelihood, going to fail chemistry. A little too little, a little too late. Report cards were being issued the following week, and I was hawking the mail like a wild man. Finally, on Wednesday of that week, my report card arrived. I stared at it for what seemed like hours. I finally said "Fuck it" and tore it open. I read left to right, then up and down. A. A. A. B.

D. Chemistry? D? I read it over and over again to make sure I was not missing anything. Nope! I got a fucking D in chemistry! I must admit, I cried like a baby. I thought for sure it was summer school for me. Brother John must have taken pity on me and gave me a D so I could graduate high school with the rest of my classmates. I love you, man! I will remember this act of kindness for the rest of my life. I even sent a message up to God that from this point on, I would never do a bad deed for the rest of my life. Please. The funniest thing was, based on how I did in my remaining classes, I'd actually made the honor roll (some of my remaining classes were advanced, so my grades were weighted heavier). How the hell does a kid make the honor roll with a D? I didn't know, and I didn't care! Life was good.

*****

This coming Friday was prom. Of course, I'd asked Nancy, my girlfriend, to join me. I was not one for these kinds of events, but it was my senior prom. I had to attend. Reminder, up until this point, my father had *never* allowed me to drive his car. He had confirmed several months in advance that he would let me use the car to go to prom. I reminded him weekly, and he reconfirmed it would not be a problem. It was now Friday afternoon, and I was getting prepared for the evening. Prom would start at eight. I needed to pick Nancy up about six thirty, meaning I needed to be on the road by six. I shaved, showered, and put my tux on. It was 5:00 p.m., and I asked my parents how I looked.

"You look fine, with the exception of that long, scraggly hair of yours."

I laughed. They'd been on my ass for years to cut my hair short. I refused. I liked my hair long. It was my way of rebelling against the system. Besides, all my friends and heroes (rock stars) wear their hair long. Then they dropped the bomb.

"You are not to take our car unless you get your haircut."

"What? Now?" I exploded. There was no way in God's greater earth I was going to get a haircut the night of my prom. I screamed. I yelled. I begged. Nothing seemed to work. It was now a Mexican standoff. I thought to myself, *There is no way my parents are going to withhold their car on the night of my senior prom.* It was now 5:30, and nothing. I started ranting and raving again. They held firm. At five forty-five, I finally realized they were not going to give in. Left without a choice, I said, "Let's go!" And my father proceeded to drive me to the corner barbershop. He had to make sure I got it cut before he was going to turn those keys over. Asshole. I told Vince the barber to cut quickly. I had to be on the road ASAP. He cut quickly, and my dad said, "Not short enough." We did this two more times until my dad gave him the seal of approval. He handed me the keys, and I bolted out the door. I jumped into the car and hauled ass north to picked up Nancy.

As she answered the door, she did a double take. She could hardly believe it was me. Her parents came to the living room and couldn't believe their eyes as well. I actually saw a big smile on her mother's face. I knew what she was thinking. *Now that's how a young man is supposed to look!* We took a few pictures and headed west to the Arlington Hilton. There were a few things that came into play this evening. One, Nancy's parents were very strict, and she had a set curfew, even for prom. She needed to be home at 11:00 p.m. sharp. Ridiculous, but such was life. The other thing was, Ricky and I hated any kind of formal shit, including prom. We couldn't get out of there fast enough. We ate, we took our prom pictures, we danced the first dance, and we were gone! We were determined to go down by Lake Michigan to spend the rest of our night looking out onto the lake and drink some champagne. Of course, we got lost, and the drive took much longer than expected. The clock was racing toward 11:00 p.m. We got down there with just enough time to have a glass of champagne, take a quick peek at the water, and take off. I got Nancy home at 11:10 p.m. Even though it was my prom night, her mother was still pissed off she was late. She laid into Nancy (speaking Polish, of course) while I stood there like an idiot. I said my goodbyes and reminded Nancy that we were spending the following day with Ricky and his girlfriend (Michele).

Ricky had an eight-man rubber dinghy. I had a case of beer. We were going to spend the day out on that dinghy, drinking beer and shooting the shit. Saturday morning came, and I asked my dad for the keys. He looked at me inquisitively and asked why I needed the keys. I reminded him of the thousand conversations we had about this particular weekend. He played dumb and said he knew nothing about it.

"Besides, me and your mother have plans for later on today."

WTF? Not again! We went back and forth for what seemed like an hour. After much debate, he reluctantly agreed to give me the keys. Thank God. I picked up Nancy, met up with Ricky and Michele, and we all headed to the lake. As we drove, I filled Nancy in on our plans. She reminded me that she did not know how to swim and was scared shitless of boats and water. Goddamn! I forgot all about that. I assured her she would be safe and that everything would be all right. We arrived at the lake and proceeded to pump up the dinghy. Of course, Nancy was even more nervous seeing we were going to be on a dinghy rather than a wooden boat.

"What if it springs a leak?"

After five minutes of back-and-forth with her, she reluctantly climbed aboard. I grabbed the case of beer, and the four of us pushed off from shore. We paddled out to the middle of the lake. I took one of the six-packs, tied it to a rope, and slung it over the side. Our anchor. We all peeled off our clothes to reveal our bathing suits. Nancy remained nervous but was a real trooper. The more we drank, the more relaxed we became. We spent a beautiful day out on the lake, catching some rays and a nice buzz. What better way to end the school year than with a day like this, spending time with my best friend Ricky, Michele, and my girlfriend Nancy? Life was good!

*****

The following week was graduation. The ceremony would be held at the Arie Crown Theater in downtown Chicago. It was a very fancy place, located right on the shores of Lake Michigan. I really didn't want to attend the ceremony, but my parents were insistent of seeing their oldest son graduate. I reluctantly agreed just to keep the peace. The truce held up until the morning of my graduation. I got up, showered, and tossed on a pair of shorts, a T-shirt, and my gym shoes. As I hit the kitchen and told my parents I was ready to go, they of course exploded.

"No son of mine is going to graduation dressed like that!"

I reminded them that I didn't want to go to this dumbass ceremony in the first place. They turned up the volume.

"Over my dead body will you be going anywhere in shorts and a T-shirt!"

Of course, I replied, "Fuck you! Let me remind you that I paid for the last two years of high school, and you can't tell me what to do!"

More cursing. More slapping. The Mexican standoff had begun once again, only this time, I held all the cards. I *was not* giving in. What was my punishment? I won't attend my graduation? Good! I didn't want to go in the first place. As the clock ticked, the negotiations began. My parents wanted me in a suit and tie. I was fine in my grubs. After much back-and-forth, I reluctantly agreed to put on a button-down shirt, a pair of blue jeans, and my cowboy boots (which I have been wearing for years by now). As it turned out, the gown I must wear hung all the way to the floor. You could have gone naked, and no one would have been the wiser. I went through the ceremony and tore off my gown as soon as we hit the exit. I was free! High school was in the rearview mirror, and we had the whole summer ahead of us. More time to fuck around with my friends, do some drinking, and cause more trouble! At this particular point in time, college seemed like light-years away. God knows what craziness lay ahead for me. Life was good!